U.S. DISENGAGEMENT FROM LATIN AMERICA: COMPROMISED SECURITY AND ECONOMIC INTERESTS

HEARING

BEFORE THE

SUBCOMMITTEE ON THE WESTERN HEMISPHERE

OF THE

COMMITTEE ON FOREIGN AFFAIRS HOUSE OF REPRESENTATIVES

ONE HUNDRED THIRTEENTH CONGRESS

SECOND SESSION

MARCH 25, 2014

Serial No. 113–136

Printed for the use of the Committee on Foreign Affairs

Available via the World Wide Web: http://www.foreignaffairs.house.gov/ or http://www.gpo.gov/fdsys/

U.S. GOVERNMENT PRINTING OFFICE

87–335PDF   WASHINGTON : 2014

For sale by the Superintendent of Documents, U.S. Government Printing Office
Internet: bookstore.gpo.gov   Phone: toll free (866) 512–1800; DC area (202) 512–1800
Fax: (202) 512–2104   Mail: Stop IDCC, Washington, DC 20402–0001

COMMITTEE ON FOREIGN AFFAIRS

EDWARD R. ROYCE, California, *Chairman*

CHRISTOPHER H. SMITH, New Jersey	ELIOT L. ENGEL, New York
ILEANA ROS-LEHTINEN, Florida	ENI F.H. FALEOMAVAEGA, American
DANA ROHRABACHER, California	Samoa
STEVE CHABOT, Ohio	BRAD SHERMAN, California
JOE WILSON, South Carolina	GREGORY W. MEEKS, New York
MICHAEL T. McCAUL, Texas	ALBIO SIRES, New Jersey
TED POE, Texas	GERALD E. CONNOLLY, Virginia
MATT SALMON, Arizona	THEODORE E. DEUTCH, Florida
TOM MARINO, Pennsylvania	BRIAN HIGGINS, New York
JEFF DUNCAN, South Carolina	KAREN BASS, California
ADAM KINZINGER, Illinois	WILLIAM KEATING, Massachusetts
MO BROOKS, Alabama	DAVID CICILLINE, Rhode Island
TOM COTTON, Arkansas	ALAN GRAYSON, Florida
PAUL COOK, California	JUAN VARGAS, California
GEORGE HOLDING, North Carolina	BRADLEY S. SCHNEIDER, Illinois
RANDY K. WEBER SR., Texas	JOSEPH P. KENNEDY III, Massachusetts
SCOTT PERRY, Pennsylvania	AMI BERA, California
STEVE STOCKMAN, Texas	ALAN S. LOWENTHAL, California
RON DeSANTIS, Florida	GRACE MENG, New York
DOUG COLLINS, Georgia	LOIS FRANKEL, Florida
MARK MEADOWS, North Carolina	TULSI GABBARD, Hawaii
TED S. YOHO, Florida	JOAQUIN CASTRO, Texas
LUKE MESSER, Indiana	

AMY PORTER, *Chief of Staff*   THOMAS SHEEHY, *Staff Director*

JASON STEINBAUM, *Democratic Staff Director*

————

SUBCOMMITTEE ON THE WESTERN HEMISPHERE

MATT SALMON, Arizona, *Chairman*

CHRISTOPHER H. SMITH, New Jersey	ALBIO SIRES, New Jersey
ILEANA ROS-LEHTINEN, Florida	GREGORY W. MEEKS, New York
MICHAEL T. McCAUL, Texas	ENI F.H. FALEOMAVAEGA, American
JEFF DUNCAN, South Carolina	Samoa
RON DeSANTIS, Florida	THEODORE E. DEUTCH, Florida
	ALAN GRAYSON, Florida

(II)

CONTENTS

(III)

U.S. DISENGAGEMENT FROM LATIN AMERICA: COMPROMISED SECURITY AND ECONOMIC INTERESTS

TUESDAY, MARCH 25, 2014

HOUSE OF REPRESENTATIVES,
SUBCOMMITTEE ON THE WESTERN HEMISPHERE,
COMMITTEE ON FOREIGN AFFAIRS,
Washington, DC.

The subcommittee met, pursuant to notice, at 3:10 p.m., in room 2255 Rayburn House Office Building, Hon. Matt Salmon (chairman of the subcommittee) presiding.

Mr. SALMON. We have kept everybody waiting for quite some time and so without objection, with unanimous consent, a quorum being present, the subcommittee will come to order, and I am going to start by recognizing myself, since I am the only one here, and then I believe the ranking member will be coming as well.

We just had a series of votes on the floor and it is that time of year. But without objection, the members of the subcommittee can submit their opening remarks for the record and I am going to yield myself as much time as I may consume to present an opening statement.

Good afternoon and welcome to this hearing where we will have the opportunity to discuss the United States' disengagement from Latin America, and what the long and short term implications are of that disengagement.

Just 2 weeks ago, Secretary of State John Kerry testified before the full Foreign Affairs Committee on the State Department's Fiscal Year 2015 budget where he failed to even mention the Western Hemisphere, our hemisphere, in his opening remarks.

The point that I made to the Secretary was that the administration needs to come up with a coherent strategy for the region, one that considers our national security and commercial interests, and one that celebrates and supports the aspirations of individuals seeking liberty and the respect of democratic principles.

The Secretary's failure to even mention our own hemisphere is particularly disconcerting when we consider everything that is going on in the region—the fact that Cuba continues to repress its people and and has been caught violating U.N. sanctions and shipping weapons to North Korea through the Panama Canal, that Venezuelan President Maduro has been violently crushing legitimate democratic protests, the wave of antagonism to us and our interests emanating from Ecuador, Bolivia and elsewhere that our strategic adversaries such as Russia, Iran and China have taken of note—taken note of our absence in the region and are establishing footholds right here in our neighborhood.

Instead of addressing this strategic failure, the administration is focused on climate change initiatives, funding solar panel projects in the highlands regions of Guatemala and elsewhere on the taxpayer's dime.

Sadly, when I mentioned these concerns to Secretary Kerry, he spent his entire time pontificating about the environment in the Pacific Islands and a typhoon in the Philippines, further making my point that we are taking our eye off the ball on the Western Hemisphere and focusing on other things and, clearly, showing a lack of strategy for the Western Hemisphere.

Not one word in his response to me about the Western Hemisphere. So I have convened today's hearing because I am deeply concerned about the administration's neglect affecting our commercial interests in that region and undermining our ability to defend liberty and economic freedom for those in Cuba, Venezuela and elsewhere where basic democratic rights have been taken away in exchange for statism and authoritarianism.

I am also concerned that our disengagement has invited the likes of Russia to increase foreign military sales while establishing strategic bases in Venezuela, Nicaragua and Cuba. It has allowed Iran to build its diplomatic and cultural presence in an effort to skirt sanctions and establish a presence close to our borders.

These realities should be the foremost on our minds of our foreign policy makers at the State Department, more so, I dare say, than the prospect of climate change.

And I don't say that to denigrate the concern for proper stewardship of our environment. I think we all care about that. It is about priorities. It is a major policy failure, I believe, of this administration to prioritize climate change projects over our strategic and diplomatic posture in the Western Hemisphere, and it is shameful for us to stand by and watch the violations of basic human rights and democratic values seen in Venezuela because of the naive belief by this administration that the OAS or other multilateral organizations can be counted on even one time to defend freedom where it is being threatened.

Secretary Kerry showcased this naivete when he announced the end of Monroe Doctrine before the OAS late last year, subjugating U.S. vital interests in the region to the whims of an organization that has long been hijacked by the anti-democratic populace of the hemisphere.

I am looking forward to hearing from our witnesses today. Ambassador Reich, I deeply respect you and I appreciate your service as our Ambassador to Venezuela. I believe you understand better than most the corroding effect on democratic values that the Bolivarian Revolution has had on the region.

Mr. Ilan Berman, who will testify to the presence of external actors establishing a presence in our hemisphere, and Mr. Claver-Carone, who has studied what has been best described to me as Cuban cancer that metastasized around the region, creating anti-democratic environments in certain parts of Latin America where freedom of expression and basic democratic values are systematically being violated.

I focus most of my attention as chairman of this subcommittee on the positive developments coming out of the hemisphere—the Pacific Alliance, growing trade and investment opportunities in Mexico, Peru and elsewhere, and the real and important prospect of energy security and independence in North America.

However, we will squander those opportunities if we continue to neglect the region through lack of sound, strategic policy, policy that reflects this country's commitment to the defense of liberty and economic freedom, and our willingness to defend those values and our vital national interests.

As I said to Secretary Kerry when he was up on the Hill 2 weeks ago, around the world and, indeed, even in our own hemisphere, liberty and economic freedom are being threatened by tyrants.

People yearning for freedom are looking to the U.S. for our leadership in defense of liberty, but instead, this administration is offering solar panels through costly USAID projects.

This is an affront to the U.S. taxpayer and an insult to those seeking freedom. We can and we must do much better. I am eager to hear how the lack of U.S. strategy and leadership in the Western Hemisphere has affected our ability to defend these values, while protecting our interests and the interests of our neighbors.

In the coming weeks, this subcommittee will have the opportunity to question the administration more directly about Western Hemisphere policy or lack thereof during a budget oversight hearing.

What we glean from your testimony today, Ambassador Reich, Mr. Berman, Mr. Claver-Carone and Mr. Shifter, will be instrumental in our ability to challenge the administration's lack of strategic vision and offer a new way forward.

I don't typically get negative in these kinds of hearings but I am really disgusted, I am, by the lack of any kind of clear vision or policy in the Western Hemisphere. And while I talk about this whole movement in the Western Hemisphere toward more climate change issues, I am not against talking about environmental policies at work.

I think that is prudent and smart. But on the scale of priorities, when we are looking at people being killed in the streets in Venezuela, when we look at arms being smuggled by Cuba to North Korea, on the relative scale of what is important are we really focusing our attention on the things that really matter? That is why we are holding this hearing today.

It is not just to cast aspersions, but to actually try to find a way that we can engage together to try to focus on our own neighborhood and make things better for all concerned, and I yield to the ranking member.

Mr. SIRES. Thank you, Mr. Chairman.

Good afternoon, and thank you to the witnesses for being here. Thank you for your patience with our vote.

I believe it is fair to acknowledge that the number, nature and complexity of foreign policy challenges facing the United States today is the greatest it has been since 9/11.

For the past 13 years our foreign policy mostly focused on crises outside our hemisphere. This is perhaps no less true today where in Eastern Europe we have Russia acting as if the Cold War had never ended.

As foreign challenges have evolved, so too have our diplomatic, economic, and when necessary, our military means to respond. Nonetheless, this focus elsewhere, however understatable, has come at the detriment of our policy toward the Americas and the hemisphere as a whole.

As a consequence, we have not paid appropriate attention to an area that is next door in our hemisphere. Human rights abuses, intimidation, threats to democracy or loss of life are no less relevant and just as wrong whether they occur in Syria, North Korea, 90 miles south in Havana or in Venezuela.

Some experts view U.S. foreign policy toward Latin America as adrift and far too narrow in scope. I agree that our problems have risen. Our responses have been reactive rather than proactive.

As bearer of democracy, liberty and economic freedom we have failed when our foreign policy is dictated by yesterday's news headlines. On one hand, today all nations in the hemisphere, with the exception of Cuba, are elected democracies.

On the other, we have witnessed a proliferation of electoral authoritism where democratic institutions exist but are severely abused by the executive.

We see this specifically in countries like Venezuela, Ecuador, Bolivia and Nicaragua. We have also witnessed a unique period of political stability and economic vibrancy that has translated to greater regional autonomy with a diverse economic and diplomatic portfolio. Foreign actors such as China, India and Europe have now become significant trading partners for some of Latin America's largest economies.

There are new regional associations such as ALBA, the Bolivarian Alliance for the Peoples of Our America-People's Trade Treaty, and CELAC, the Community of Latin American and Caribbean States, that not only exclude the United States but have mostly been utilized as mediums to espouse and advocate anti-Americanism.

Russia has dubiously increased military exercises in the region and Iran continues to expand its influence. While such an agreement should never have come to light, President Kirchner's decision to undo the so-called joint truth commission with Iran is a step in the right direction.

I am adamant the U.S. must maintain pressure on Cuba's authoritative regime, expose its continued human rights and press freedom violations, blatant disregard for U.N. arms sanctions and press for the release of Alan Gross.

In regards to Venezuela, I have joined my colleagues in calling for an end to violence in supporting the people of Venezuela's right to express their frustration to the deteriorating economy, public safety and political conditions in their country.

Rather than allow the space and freedom for peaceful demonstration, President Maduro has instead utilized oppressive Cuban tactics in silencing the media, detaining anti-government demonstrators and opposing leaders.

Mr. Maduro and the Government of Venezuela need to address the grievances of its people through dialogue, and respect freedom of expression and assembly as the basic human rights and principles of a democratic society.

It is unacceptable that various member states of the OAS who champion their respects of human and civil rights have chosen to ignore the abuses occurring in Venezuela and have prevented the OAS from taking any meaningful action against the Government of Venezuela.

These nations value Venezuela's cheap oil and petrol dollars more than human rights and the unfortunate loss of life that has occurred. To the leaders of these nations, I say that the world is watching, and that the U.S. and this Congress, in particular, will not forget.

I call on the administration to utilize and exhaust all diplomatic and economic tools at its disposal to act accordingly against those individuals responsible for the unnecessary and unwarranted acts of violence against the Venezuelan people.

U.S. inaction will speak louder than any anti-America rhetoric espoused by blind nations on the wrong side of history. Thank you.

Mr. SALMON. Thank you. Mr. Duncan.

Mr. DUNCAN. Just real briefly, first off I will say that I share the chairman's opinion that this is Venezuela's 1776 moment where you have a people that are urging and really yearning to be free and have more self-governance.

But when we witnessed, just recently, President Maduro encouraging Venezuelan citizens to begin Carnival early while thousands stood in line for the basic subsistence which they would have trouble finding on the grocery shelves, this likened sort of to Marie Antoinette's ''let them eat cake'' statement.

It shows how out of touch Maduro is with just the basic needs of the Venezuelans. So maybe history will show that this is Maduro's ''let them eat cake'' moment and hopefully we as Americans can support the folks that want to be free, and want to govern themselves and Venezuela.

So I thank the gentlemen for being here. I know this isn't just focused on Venezuela but that is what is on my mind today. I yield back.

Mr. SALMON. Thank you. Mr. Meeks.

Mr. MEEKS. Thank you, Mr. Chairman. And let me just say that this is a timely discussion and I want to thank the witnesses that are here and look forward to having a dialogue with you, doing the questions and answers and hearing your testimony.

I got elected to Congress in 1998, and from 1998 until today I have long said that we have not engaged Latin America, South America, the Caribbean, and Central America in the methods that we should.

Oftentimes we looked at our friends, our neighbors to the south in the manner that we were looking through the prism of when we were in the Cold War, that we had not changed many of our policies toward them, that we had not moved forward and we were not engaged with them and that we needed to focus on our neighbors to the south because they are our neighbors.

We share this hemisphere. They are very important, and if we didn't do it then others would come and they would try to invest and influence and be involved in their matters because we are leaving a vacuum, and that the nations in Central and South America were looking for different types of relationships, not a master-servant relationship but a relationship where they were recognized for growing and moving and trying to move toward democracy and making sure that all people within those communities and within those countries will have an opportunity to have their voices heard, not just someone to be utilized by us when we thought that it would be to our strategic interest.

We still need to be sure that we are engaging with our colleagues and our friends and our neighbors who share this hemisphere with us. It is absolutely important and we must talk to them, not at them, so that we can begin to figure out how we can work collectively together to make this hemisphere better.

Otherwise, others will take advantage. Others will try to divide the hemisphere. It can then cause us to have some national security interests.

So I was pleased when we have had conferences that I have attended and seen the nations come and we have had various groups going to talk and to try to figure out how do we do this thing.

How do we work in a manner of bringing folks together, of understanding to some degree some different ethnicities, some different histories, so that we can work together to make our hemisphere stronger.

So I say that is why I think that if we are going to have a real dialogue, and I probably differ than many when I see, I believe, a failed policy with reference to one of the Caribbean countries for over 50 years, I want that regime to change. But I want something that works because it hasn't. I think the time for that conversation is to be had.

How do we make effective change and how do we work together to get it done? So I look forward to hearing the testimony. I look forward to working with my colleagues who all, I believe, have good intentions and want to make sure that we have a good relationship with many of the countries in the hemisphere so that we can make a difference. I think the time has finally come.

The time is right for us to do it and I look forward to working collectively to get it done, and I yield back.

Thank you.

Mr. SALMON. Thank you.

I recognize the gentlewoman from Florida, Ms. Ileana Ros-Lehtinen.

Ms. ROS-LEHTINEN. Thank you so much, Mr. Chairman.

And I, like so many of our colleagues here, am extremely worried about our lack of attention to the many threats to democracy in our own hemisphere.

In Venezuela, the death toll is at 34, and continues to climb with nearly 60 reported cases of torture, over 1,500 people unjustly detained, hundreds more injured, and the nexus between Cuba and Venezuela continues to threaten regional stability. It frightens freedom-loving people who are risking their lives for liberty, for democracy, and for justice.

The Castro brothers continue to aid and abet the Maduro regime just as they have aided and abetted the FARC guerillas in Colombia, and now they are pulling off this farce of peace negotiations in Cuba and have been carrying out systematic human rights abuses, and incarcerating opposition leaders, and that same coalition has had a stranglehold, lamentably so, on the OAS—the Organization for American States.

They have bullied member states into acquiescence. On Friday, as you know, Mr. Chairman, the OAS, led by the ALBA group, silenced a Venezuelan legislator and one of the leading opposition leaders, María Corina Machado, prevented her from speaking the truth.

María Corina sought to denounce the human rights abuses occurring in Venezuela but this broken institution, led by a cowardly Secretary General, chose to side with Maduro instead and yet just 2 weeks ago Secretary Kerry testified in front of our full committee that we need to work closely with the OAS in support of democracy in Venezuela, and the OAS was capitulating to Maduro and the Castros on Friday and throughout the years, this ordinary session silencing the truth of what is happening in Venezuela just a few blocks from the White House, and the administration continued to say that the OAS believes in what we believe in.

And I believe, Mr. Chairman, the inmates are, clearly, running the asylum in the OAS. We are talking about a Maduro regime that is incarcerating opposition leaders, that is killing young people in the streets. María Corina may very well, because her immunity has been voided, she could be arrested.

She could be imprisoned under false pretenses, tried for treason for daring to try to speak at the OAS, and on Cuba the State Department has been trying so hard to approve more visas for Castro lackeys and finding new ways to inject money in the coffers of the Castro brothers that it has not observed the sad reality that the Cuban people are suffering day in and day out.

The OAS has failed to be a venue for the people of Venezuela, for the people of Cuba, the people of the hemisphere to express their concerns about the lack of democracy and the violations of human rights occurring in our hemisphere every day.

Thank you very much, Mr. Chairman.

Mr. SALMON. In the interests of time, if it is all right with you we will just dispense with introductions. Pursuant to Committee Rule 7, the members of the subcommittee will be permitted to submit written statements to be included in the official hearing record, and without objection the hearing record will remain open for 7 days to allow opening statements, questions and extraneous materials for the record subject to the length of limitation in the rules.

I am going to start with you, Ambassador Reich.

STATEMENT OF THE HONORABLE OTTO J. REICH, PRESIDENT, OTTO REICH ASSOCIATES, LLC

Ambassador REICH. Thank you, Mr. Chairman, members of the subcommittee, Chairman Emeritus Ros-Lehtinen. It is good to be here. I appreciate the opportunity to address this very important issue. I will not be following my written testimony but will summarize it for you.

That we have neglected the hemisphere is not in question. All one has to do is travel in the region and we will be asked why the U.S. doesn't care about Latin America or the Caribbean.

That disengagement carries real cost for the United States in political, economic, security and commercial terms, especially when it is accompanied by misguided policies that have confused our friends and emboldened our enemies.

Believing that just by sitting down to talk with our antagonists they will stop their hostility is not diplomacy. It is self-delusion. As relations with Russia, North Korea, Syria and Iran prove, wishful thinking does not make an effective foreign policy.

The same goes for the Americas. At its outset, the Obama administration unilaterally lifted travel and financial sanctions on Cuba and offered a diplomatic reset to Venezuela, Bolivia, Ecuador and other anti-American governments.

For example, the administration inexplicably joined Castro, Chávez, Ortega and the OAS in trying to reinstate Honduras' radical and corrupt President, Manuel Zelaya, to the presidency even after Zelaya had been legally dismissed by the Supreme Court of Honduras and their Parliament for violating the constitution.

What was the reaction from our adversaries? Castro, Chá vez, Maduro, Correa, Morales, Ortega and even Argentina's Kirchner variously at times have intensified their ties with Russia, Belarus, Iran, Syria, Hezbollah, purchased Russian weapons, expelled American officials, put independent news organizations out of business and generally undermined liberties at home.

Castro responded to the lifting of sanctions by increasing internal repression and jailing a U.S. citizen on trumped-up charges. Cuba was later caught helping North Korea to violate U.N. sanctions on weapons transfers.

Further confusing our friends, the administration delayed for 3 years the ratification of free trade agreements with Colombia and Panama while slowing the implementation of the Merida Initiative, an anti-narcotics program with Mexico.

Our disengagement is evident at the Organization of American States where this month alone a majority of the members voted to support Maduro's violent repression. One economic consequence of U.S. policy is an uneven playing field where U.S. firms cannot win some major contracts in Latin America because their competitors are bribing foreign decision makers.

This is one result of our Government not implementing our own visa sanctions against corrupt officials coming to the U.S., opening bank accounts and owning property here.

We must pay special attention to Cuba and Venezuela since these two countries have provided most of the muscle and money for the anti-American subversion of the past 15 years. Cuba is a totalitarian military dictatorship controlled by the Communist Party of Cuba.

It is on the State Department's list of state sponsors of terrorism and is run by an organized crime family whose head, Fidel Castro, has made so much money he was listed on Forbes register of the world's richest people.

The Castros have been involved in illicit businesses such as narcotics trafficking, kidnapping, bank robbery and money laundering.

With the help of Hugo Chávez and later Nicolás Maduro, Castro has remade Venezuela in his image.

This is not just my opinion. Listen to what Chávez's one-time ideological mentor and main cabinet minister, Luis Miquilena, said recently:

> "Venezuela today is a country that is practically occupied by the henchmen of two international criminals—Cuba's Castro brothers. They have introduced in Venezuela a true army of occupation. The Cubans run the maritime ports, airports, communications, the most essential issues in Venezuela. We are in the hands of a foreign country."

By Cuba, Venezuela has become an organized crime state. Politicians and military officers have been implicated in drug trafficking, support of terrorism and other illicit activities. Corruption runs rampant with huge fortunes illegally acquired by government officials and the so-called oligarchy.

The U.S. Treasury Department has designated a dozen senior Venezuelan officials as "significant foreign narcotics trafficker" under the Drug Kingpin Act. They stand accused of "materially assisting the narcotics trafficking activities" of the revolutionary armed forces of Colombia, the FARC, designated as a foreign terrorist organization by the State Department and European counterparts.

Under the influence of the Cuba-Venezuela alliance, ALBA, which has been mentioned here along with other anti-American governments are repressing their populations, eliminating free enterprise, destroying press freedoms and other liberties and supporting terrorists and racketeers.

Moreover, they are now bringing their illicit activities to the United States. To prevent what Mr. Miquilena correctly calls criminals, from consolidating their dictatorships or exporting violence, we must actively defend our interests and our security.

This does not entail military force. One of our most effective tools and one that the U.S. is finally using against the Russian oligarchs as a result of the Crimea annexation are targeted visa and financial sanctions aimed at those government officials who repress their people and of the business accomplices who help keep the dictatorships in power and who profit from its corruption.

Also, instead of constantly putting out fires in our neighborhood, we should put the arsonists out of business. The chief arsonist in this hemisphere for the past half century has been a Castro. We know where he lives and where he hides his money.

Thank you.

[The prepared statement of Ambassador Reich follows:]

Testimony of
The Hon. Otto J. Reich
President, Otto Reich Associates, LLC
Presented Before the House Committee on Foreign Affairs
March 25, 2014
"US Disengagement from Latin America: Compromised
Security and Economic Interests."

Mr. Chairman and Members of the Committee: I thank you
for the opportunity to come before this Committee once
again to address a phenomenon that, if ignored, could
threaten the security of our country: the increasing anti-
Americanism and radicalization of some governments in the
region, and the lack of effective response by our government.

In the past few years the US government has neglected parts
of the western hemisphere while adopting a misguided
approach toward others. For example, in 2009 the Obama
Administration seemed more determined to reach out to
unfriendly governments such as Cuba, Venezuela, Bolivia,
and Ecuador, than to friendlier states, such as Mexico,
Colombia, Peru and Chile. That sent confusing signals to
friend and foe alike.

Some say that the Administration believed that if it could get
our adversaries to just listen to our earnest message, then
they would stop their hostile behavior. That is not
diplomacy; that is self-delusion. As we have seen with
Russia, North Korea, Syria and Iran, wishful thinking does
not make for an effective foreign policy. The same reasoning
applies in our part of the world.

For example, in its first year in office the Obama
Administration unilaterally lifted financial sanctions against
the military dictatorship in Cuba, thus allowing the Castro

brothers to capture several billion dollars per year in travel and remittances that had been previously denied their regime. It offered Venezuela's Hugo Chavez and Bolivia's Evo Morales a clean slate and exchange of Ambassadors; it later sent Secretary of State Hillary Clinton to Ecuador to dine with and convince President Rafael Correa to tone down his anti-Americanism.

What the Administration received in return for this outreach was rejection and disappointment. Chavez and later his successor Nicolas Maduro continued their harsh anti-American actions and rhetoric, their close ties with Iran, Syria, and Hezbollah, their purchases of Russian weapons, their four billion dollar subsidies of Castro's Cuba, their relentless march toward a closed society in Cuba's image. Ecuador's Correa similarly rejected US entreaties: he closed the US anti-narcotics monitoring base at Manta, expelled the American Ambassador and other diplomats, put independent news outlets out of business through threats and lawsuits, and directed his cousin Pedro Delgado, the head of the Central Bank, to establish covert business ties with Russia and Iran, which included opening secret bank accounts in Moscow and meetings with Iranian officials in both Tehran and Quito.

For months in 2009 the Obama Administration tried to have Honduras' Manuel Zelaya, an ally of Hugo Chavez, Fidel Castro and Daniel Ortega, and whom had been accused of corruption and of violating national laws, restored to the presidency, even though Zelaya had been removed from office for violating Honduras' constitution by a unanimous vote of that nation's Supreme Court, a decision that was subsequently ratified by nine of every ten members of Honduras' National Assembly.

Conversely, in the same year of 2009 the Administration inexplicably slowed down the implementation of the Merida Initiative, a collaborative anti-narcotics program with Mexico whose success holds obvious benefits for both our countries. In addition, the Administration waited nearly three years to submit to Congress the Free Trade Agreements (FTA) with Colombia and Panama, and then only after pressure from this Congress, which held hostage Administration nominees and legislative initiatives. By delaying policy initiatives with such obvious benefit to the US and its friends as the FTA's, the Merida Initiative and others, while offering unearned favors to our adversaries, the Administration's policy has confused our friends and emboldened our enemies.

The Administration unwisely believes that the Castro brothers will see our generosity as a sign of good will, not realizing that they run the island as the Mafia runs its enterprises, and that they therefore saw these offerings as a desire by the US to overlook Cuba's 5 decades of anti-Americanism, internal repression and sponsorship of international terrorism. Regardless of what self-professed experts in US universities or think tanks may say, the Castro brothers know very well that for the past 55 years they have engaged in some of the most criminal, violent and illicit activities of any nation across three continents - and they know that we know it.

So, imagine the Castro brothers' glee when the new President of the US, while getting nothing in return, grants them an unexpected windfall: the ability to capture billions of US dollars from overseas relatives of their captive island population, who send money or travel to the island to visit family that cannot leave. Naturally, Castro responded to President Obama's magnanimity by increasing repression against peaceful dissidents in Cuba and by arresting a US citizen on trumped-up charges, holding a kangaroo trial in which he was sentenced to 15 years in jail for taking – on behalf of the US Agency for International Development – commercial computer and telephone equipment to the remnants of the Jewish community in Cuba so they could communicate with the outside world. To add insult to injury, the Castro government and its apologists are suggesting that the hostage aid worker be exchanged for Cuban intelligence agents duly convicted in US court of espionage against US military installations.

The Castro's saw the Obama Administration's removal of sanctions as a sign of the acceptance of their half-century of criminal activity just as they had seen the Carter Administration's similar efforts in 1977. That year President Carter renewed diplomatic relations with Castro after a 17-year hiatus; Castro then responded by increasing Cuban military support for communist guerilla movements and governments in 14 African countries.

Part of the price of US disengagement from Latin America can now be seen in such reprehensible spectacles as those witnessed this month at the Organization of American States (OAS) in which, for example, a member of the elected Venezuelan legislature representing the peaceful dissident movement and duly invited by an OAS Member State, was not allowed to speak, while earlier a majority of the OAS members voted to support the violent repression that the entire world has seen on video: uniformed soldiers, plain-clothes police and government-organized militia beating, shooting and killing unarmed civilians, mostly students and even a pregnant woman.

Another increasingly visible element of the US disengagement has been the unwillingness to confront the rampant official corruption that prohibits legitimate US businesses from winning contracts because their competitors routinely bribe foreign officials responsible for the awards. This corruption is not limited to anti-American nations; it takes place in far too many countries, some of which pretend to be pro-free market and profess friendship with the US. Although corruption is non-ideological, it has particularly thrived in those countries whose governments have consolidated power and decision-making in hands of a few privileged anti-American populists. Corruption has grown in those countries because their rulers have eliminated the free press that serves as a watchdog of government abuse while at the same time politicizing the judiciary which no longer acts as an arbiter of justice but rather as a defender of the government and the powerful.

We may better understand the current situation in Latin America by focusing on the relationship between Cuba and Venezuela, the two countries that have been respectively providing the ideological and financial resources for most of the recent anti-American trend. What we see happening in Venezuela and elsewhere is largely due to Cuba transforming Venezuela into its mirror image and to the US largely ignoring it.

It is worth restating that Cuba is a totalitarian military dictatorship, a one-party state controlled by the Communist Party of Cuba, listed on the US State Department's list of State Sponsors of Terrorism, and run for 55 years by an organized crime family whose patriarch, Fidel Castro, has become so wealthy that he was catalogued on Forbes' list of the "World's Richest People."

The Castro family rules Cuba through the usual mechanisms of a totalitarian dictatorship, including: absolute control of all branches of government, the Armed Forces and the police; violent repression of any dissidence to include assassination; excessive prison terms under inhuman conditions; unrestricted surveillance of all citizens; state ownership of the means of production and distribution; and complete lack of the individual liberties guaranteed by the Universal Declaration of the Rights of Man, of which Cuba is, of course, a non-compliant signatory.

Throughout the Americas, Cuba's ruling family has been involved in illicit business such as narcotics trafficking, kidnapping, bank robbery, and money laundering. By his own admission, Castro has trained and supported terrorists for what he calls "wars of national liberation" in every corner of the western hemisphere. It is his willingness to use mobster tactics against his adversaries that has protected Castro from criticism by democratic leaders; most of whom are afraid to suffer the fate of those whom Castro has singled out for punishment (one of the first targets was the then-president of Venezuela, Romulo Betancourt, in the early 1960's, who refused Castro's attempted extortion).

Although Cuba never stopped exporting its model of one-party dictatorship to Latin America, it has changed its methods. Until the end of the massive Soviet economic subsidies in 1989, it supported revolution through armed means. When the USSR disappeared and Chavez's money replaced the USSR's, Castro switched to supporting a much more deceptive and therefore insidious method: supporting allies who could win a democratic election, and then changing the rules so that there would never again be another free and fair election in the ally's "socialist" country. That is what we are seeing today in the ALBA alliance created by Fidel Castro and Hugo Chavez, in the so-called "21st Century Socialist States" such as Ecuador, Bolivia, Nicaragua and Venezuela. That is what we might have seen in Honduras had the Administration not seen the error of its policy and reversed course with Zelaya. However, we may still see this occur in El Salvador, with the recent election to the presidency of a former top commander of the Marxist-Leninist FMLN guerrilla army who has been implicated in numerous assassinations during the war and the official corruption of the current FMLN government.

From the start of his 14 years in power in Venezuela, Hugo Chavez willingly turned over to Fidel Castro the management of much of Venezuela's national security and the fruits of its oil revenues. You don't have to take my word for it. Last month the man that has been called Chavez's ideological mentor and most important Cabinet Minister, Luis Miquilena, said:

"Venezuela today is a country that is practically occupied by the henchmen of two international criminals, Cuba's Castro brothers. They have introduced in Venezuela a true army of occupation. The Cubans run the maritime ports, airports, communications, the most essential issues in Venezuela. We are in the hands of a foreign country." [**El Nacional**, 3/4/13]

Under Venezuela's Constitution, the Minister of Interior is not only in charge of all internal security, but also served as Acting President in the absence of the President, for example, on the latter's international travel or temporary incapacitation. Miquilena was later head of Venezuela's National Assembly, or Congress. His opinion, therefore, carries much weight and can be equated to that of a US Vice President or Speaker of the House.

The roots of the Cuban domination of Venezuela go back to the very start of Castro's half-century rule over Cuba. On January 8, 1959, a week after the departure of the outgoing dictator, Fulgencio Batista, Castro rode into Havana atop a captured army tank. Exactly 15 days later he flew to Venezuela and asked the then-president, Romulo Betancourt, for $300 million (equivalent to about $2.5 billion today) to undermine the US in the western hemisphere. A surprised Betancourt turned Castro's request down flat, telling the Cuban that Venezuela was still a poor country in spite of its oil wealth, while Cuba was a "rich country." Castro never forgave Betancourt. Three years later Castro sent a covert military expedition against Venezuela to support a communist guerilla war against the democratically elected Betancourt government. The guerilla lasted the rest of that decade. It was not the first and would not be the last of Castro's many military interventions in Venezuela or the rest of Latin America.

Like its patron Cuba, Venezuela has also become an organized crime state. Top politicians and high-ranking military officers have been implicated in drug trafficking, support of terrorism and other illicit activities. Corruption runs rampant, with fortunes in the hundreds of millions and billions of dollars having been illegally acquired by a few well-placed government officials and their private business associates.

Again, don't take my word for it: The US Treasury Department has designated a number of senior Venezuelan officials as "Significant Foreign Narcotics Traffickers" under the Drug Kingpin Act. The individuals so accused include what in the equivalent US government position would be the US Attorney General, the Director of a combined FBI and

CIA, the Director of the Defense Intelligence Agency, the Secretary of Homeland Security and commanders of strategic military units. All stand accused of "materially assisting the narcotics trafficking activities of the FARC" the Spanish acronym for the Revolutionary Armed Forces of Colombia, a guerrilla army designated as a "Foreign Terrorist Organization" by the US State Department and European counterparts.

Other overwhelming and convincing evidence has been gathered from multiple sources to prove without doubt that some of the highest ranking officials of the Maduro and Chavez governments have supported terrorism through involvement in narcotics trafficking - just as Castro's Cuba has done and trained them to do.

Moreover, Chavez's apprentice and appointed successor, Nicolas Maduro, has been violently repressing peaceful dissent in the streets of Venezuela for all the world to see. Still there are some who defend that government. Some Hollywood celebrities still do and until recently members of this Congress did.

But the evil influence of the Cuba-Venezuela axis does not stop at its borders. Other ALBA nations and their accomplices are also repressing their populations, eliminating free enterprise, destroying press freedoms and other basic liberties, and supporting terrorists and racketeers. The illicit activities of these countries are well-known to our government but not to the vast majority of the American people. And their criminal activity is reaching our shores. Arrests have been made on US soil of agents of some of those countries, as they attempted to blackmail or extort foreign citizens that had refused to submit to their demands before seeking refuge here. They are also bringing ill-gotten money to acquire legitimate properties and businesses that would allow the culprits to launder their dirty profits in our open economy.

What should the US do:

First the good news: to turn our policy around and start supporting our friends and opposing our enemies no new budget allocations are necessary. We should:

Establish a diplomatic equivalent of the "IFF" device used on airplanes and radars. IFF stands for "Identification Friend or Foe." Our support should be reserved for our friends. Not all states are friends and we shouldn't pretend they are. Some governments, like North Korea's, Iran's, or Syria's, cannot be dealt with as if they were normal. The same can be said for Cuba and Venezuela. Unordinary conditions call for unordinary measures.

Implement a foreign policy version of the Hippocratic Code. Doctors are taught to "first, do no wrong." The US must examine its economic and political relations with the nations of this hemisphere to make sure we are not, wittingly or unwittingly, helping anti-American governments to survive the blunders of their own doing. If they are going broke because they are corrupt, are following Marxist economic policies, buying huge quantities of weapons, supporting terrorism or otherwise subverting neighboring countries, then they are most likely anti-US; do not throw them a life preserver. If we find that we are providing aid, credits, trade or immigration or any other political or economic preference to anti-US nations, we should find legal ways to reduce or eliminate them.

Once we know who they are, we must be more proactive in supporting our friends and opposing our adversaries. Notice I say proactive, not vocal: we should not engage in spitting contests with cobras or in verbal battles with deceitful Third World autocrats. But when our resources are limited it is self-defeating to treat friends and enemies alike. That is what we have done for the past few years and the result is evident in what is happening at the OAS now. A majority of member states supported Venezuela's effort to keep the people of the hemisphere's democracies from learning the truth about chavista repression.

The ALBA nations have said that they will defeat the US through "asymmetric" warfare; we should take up the challenge. They think we have no options but to either accept their imposition of neo-communist, Cuban-style dictatorships or to strike at them militarily. They reason that, since the US has a military force unequalled in the world, our use of it would represent a "lose-lose" strategy. That is, if we use military force to defeat them, then we will have lost the battle of ideas. On the other hand, if we refrain from using it, then their superior ideology will triumph.

The fact is that that their violent, dictatorial ideology is a proven failure. It failed in the 20th Century when it was called "National Socialism" in Germany and Italy, or international socialism by the Soviet Bloc. And has been a failure in the 21st Century, in Cuba, Venezuela, and any other place where individual initiative is replaced by collectivism.

Use our economic power: The reason the US is the single most successful economic power in history is because it relies on free enterprise and free individuals for economic decisions, the very freedom that those failed ideologies destroy. We should therefore not provide economic oxygen to governments that asphyxiate their own populations' freedoms.

We should use non-military instruments, not force, to ensure that they do not succeed in establishing dictatorships or exporting violence. Those instruments include: judicious use of US economic power; non-violent but imaginative intelligence activities; open, assertive engagement in the battle of information and ideas (possibly through the re-establishment of a US Information Agency). And targeted sanctions aimed at those government officials who repress their people and the business associates who help keep them in power while they profit from the autocracy's corruption.

Those corrupt officials and their private sector enablers must be the target of US anti-corruption sanctions, such as those comprised in the International Emergency Economic Powers Act; Section 212 of the Immigration and Nationality Act; Presidential Proclamation 7750 (the "anti-kleptocracy act") and other laws and regulations that are not being sufficiently enforced.

Instead of constantly trying to put out fires in our neighborhood, it would better for the US to take the matches and the gasoline away from the arsonist. The chief arsonist in the western hemisphere for the half-century has had the last name of Castro. After 55 years observing Castro destroy his own economy, enslave his people and export violence, the US Government has more than enough viable ideas as to how to stop him than I can list in this document. What has been lacking in Washington is political will.

In this hemisphere at the present time there are nine nations that have joined the Castro-Chavez alliance called ALBA (Bolivarian Alternative of Our Americas). The purpose of that group is to spread the kind of economic, political and social system that has rued Cuba for the past 55 years. Presidents of ALBA member governments, such as Ecuador's Rafael Correa, Bolivia's Evo Morales and Nicaragua's Daniel Ortega, have publicly stated their admiration for and loyalty to the ideology espoused by Castro and Chavez. Even absent their anti-US speeches, their anti-US actions speak volumes. There is no reason to continue treating those nations as though they were friendly. Again, there is no reason to undertake any war-like action against them, but at what point does their continued hostility and support for our enemies warrant a reaction?

Finally, there are those other nations like Argentina, Brazil, Dominican Republic and some the English-speaking Caribbean that have supported the Cuba-Venezuela axis on many occasions (such as at the OAS). While they have not yet actively become anti-American, they are also not defending freedom in the hemisphere. Moreover, many have some of the most corrupt governments in the region, thus shutting out US firms from domestic competition because of US laws that prohibit bribery. The laws against them are on the books; they must be enforced.

———

Mr. SALMON. Thank you.

Mr. Berman.

STATEMENT OF MR. ILAN I. BERMAN, VICE PRESIDENT, AMERICAN FOREIGN POLICY COUNCIL

Mr. BERMAN. Thank you, Mr. Chairman, and thank you for the opportunity to appear here today. Let me begin simply by making two general and rather uncomfortable observations.

The first is that Latin America does not rank on any given day very high on the list of the United States foreign policy priorities and that that is especially true today when you see international attention being rivetted to the Middle East, to Ukraine, to Crimea, and to the Indian Ocean.

But by virtue of its geography, by virtue of its strategic position and its proximity to the U.S. homeland, Latin America is important. Indeed, it is vital to the United States on both economic and security grounds.

This is, I think, a general observation that everybody understands but I don't think it can be stressed enough.

The second observation, which we are beginning to learn at our great detriment, is the fact that nature really does abhor a vacuum and a retraction of interest, a retraction of presence on the part of the United States, will inevitably be filled by others, and that is precisely what is happening today.

Even as the U.S. has disengaged systematically from the region, other actors have stepped in and done so in ways that are deeply detrimental to American security. Let me start by explaining what Russia is doing.

Russia recently announced plans and made considerable news by doing so at the end of February to establish overseas military bases in eight countries including three Latin American ones—Venezuela, Cuba and Nicaragua.

This represents a rather substantial expansion of Russian policy in the region. Over the last several years, Moscow has devoted, I would say, significant political equities to building diplomatic ties, to building economic ties and even a strategic foothold of a sort in the Americas.

Notably, in keeping with its ideology, the regimes that the Kremlin has focused on in this outreach are those that share a broad expansionist and anti-American outlook.

Moscow's attention is focused primarily, although not exclusively, on Nicaragua, on Venezuela and on Cuba, and through official visits, arms sales and military cooperation Russia has succeeded in creating what can be called legitimately a strategic beachhead in Latin America.

And this is a policy that is being driven by a number of things, some of them practical and some of them less so. The Kremlin has recently focused on counternarcotics, and pursuant to a 2013 plan that was unveiled by the Kremlin, it is in the process of expanding counternarcotics cooperation with a number of Latin American states. Nicaragua being chief among them, this has already begun to net dividends including a bust of more than $1 million that was carried out jointly by Russia and Nicaragua last year.

The Russians have also built a fairly significant arms trade relationship with the region, focusing in large part on Venezuela, which now makes up more than three quarters of the arms that Russia sells in the region to the tune of—in excess of $14 billion so far.

But above all, and I think it is useful to point out here, Russia's activities are both strategic and opportunistic. Latin America is by any measure very far outside Moscow's core areas of interest, which are the post-Soviet spaces of Central Asia and the Caucuses, the Arctic, Eastern Europe, what have you.

Latin America is very far afield. But precisely because it sees the United States withdrawing, it sees the United States, or at least perceives the United States, to be disinterested, Moscow is taking full advantage of what it now sees as an empty region.

There is a Russian adage that says that a sacred space will not remain empty for long and I think that is very much applicable not only to Latin America, but also to Latin America in terms of how Russia is approaching it.

And I would add parenthetically here that what you are seeing over the last several weeks has been a rather worrying evolution of how Russia thinks about Latin America because in the announcement that was made at the end of February by the Russian defense minister about the possibility of bases in Latin America, it was made clear that the negotiations that are now underway are to allow for aerial refuelling, for long-range reconnaissance aircraft.

This is very much a throwback to the type of activities that the Russians, at that time the Soviets, used Latin America for.

The second actor I think worth noting is Iran. We in the United States, and particularly in the Washington Beltway, have focused on Iran relatively recently. Only since the botched attempt to assassinate the Saudi Ambassador to the U.S. by Iran's Revolutionary Guards back in October 2011 has there really been sustained attention to this presence.

But the presence actually extends far further back in history, at least a decade with regard to the modern contemporary outreach that you see the Iranians carrying out, and this outreach essentially focuses along three main lines.

First, Iran sees Latin America as an arena for political and economic outreach because of the presence of sympathetic regimes in Venezuela, Bolivia, Ecuador, and elsewhere.

Second, Iran seeks to acquire strategic resources in the Americas including, but definitely not limited to, the acquisition of uranium ore for its nuclear program.

Finally, Iran has made Latin America an arena of asymmetric activity through its contacts with regional radical groups, and also by building infrastructure in the region such as the Regional Defense School for the Bolivarian Alliance of the Americas that Iran partially funded, which is located outside of Santa Cruz, Bolivia.

Iran's presence in Latin America tends to be minimized by some because its level of activity is comparatively low, and because a majority of the economic promises that it has made to regional states so far haven't materialized.

But it is useful to remember that Iran's contemporary outreach is new. It is less than a decade old and Iran is in a much, much better position strategically in Latin America than it was 10 years ago, and this is in part because the U.S. Government still does not have an implemented strategy to compete, contest, and/or dilute Iranian influence in the Americas despite the fact that it clearly constitutes an incipient threat to American interests.

Finally, let me say a couple of words about China. Unlike Iran and Russia, China's presence in the Americas is mostly economic in nature but it is significant nonetheless because China's legitimate economic outreach, and it is very significant, has been mirrored by more questionable activities including cooperation with Argentina on nuclear issues, the launch of reconnaissance satellites for Venezuela and for Bolivia, and its much discussed plan to build an alternative to the Panama Canal in Nicaragua, which is by all accounts a very costly boondoggle but also one that will provide regional regimes with the ability to skirt U.S. oversight for containers if it is concluded.

There is a commonality here between China on the one hand and Iran and Russia on the other. Beijing, like Moscow and Tehran, is seeking to take advantage of America's disengagement for the region for its own purposes, be they economic or strategic, which gets us to where we are.

As you mentioned, Mr. Chairman, last fall Secretary of State Kerry announced that the era of the Monroe Doctrine is over, effectively, in the region. By doing that, he effectively served notice to regional regimes that they are allowed to curry favor with external actors and served notice to external actors that America will no longer contest and compete with those external actors when they reach into the region.

Moscow and Tehran and Beijing were doubtless listening when the Secretary spoke and what they likely heard was an invitation to further deepen the involvement that they are already pursuing in the region.

If history is any judge, if the last decade is any judge, that deepened involvement is going to come in ways that are going to have profound security and economic implications for the United States.

Thank you.

[The prepared statement of Mr. Berman follows:]

U.S. Disengagement from Latin America: Compromised Security and Economic Interests

Testimony before the
House Foreign Relations Committee
Subcommittee on the Western Hemisphere

March 25, 2014

Ilan Berman
Vice President
American Foreign Policy Council

Chairman Salmon, Ranking member Sires, distinguished members of the Subcommittee:

Thank you for the invitation to appear before you today to discuss the current state of American policy toward Latin America, and the strategic costs that may be incurred by the United States as a result.

Any serious discussion of this subject must start by acknowledging that Latin America has historically served as a foreign policy backwater for the United States, one overshadowed by Europe, the Middle East and Asia on the agendas of successive administrations. This is deeply counterintuitive, because by virtue of their geographic proximity the countries of the Americas are natural trading partners for the United States. It is also dangerous, since the region's large ungoverned spaces and widespread anti-Americanism have the potential to breed direct threats to the United States. Indeed, the criminal gangs and drug cartels endemic to Central and South America are already viewed as top tier national security concerns by the U.S. intelligence community.[1] Nevertheless, inattention to the region remains the norm within the Washington Beltway.

This state of affairs, moreover, is worsening. Since taking office, the Obama administration has systematically disengaged from Latin America, scaling back funding for key initiatives (like the longstanding and highly-successful Plan Colombia), failing to bolster important military partnerships and arrangements, and equivocating over political developments in vulnerable regional states.[2] At the same time, budgetary cutbacks and fiscal austerity have resulted in a significant paring back of the U.S. military's presence and activities in the Americas.

America's retraction, meanwhile, has been mirrored by the regional advance of three other significant strategic actors.

RUSSIA'S RETURN

In recent weeks, international attention has been riveted by Russia's neo-imperial efforts in Ukraine—steps which have raised the specter of a new Cold War between Moscow and the West. In the process, another alarming facet of the Kremlin's contemporary foreign policy has gone largely unnoticed: its growing military presence in, and strategic designs on, the Western Hemisphere.

On February 26th, Russian Defense Minister Sergei Shoigu formally announced his government's plan to expand its overseas military presence. Russia, Mr. Shoigu outlined, intends to establish new military bases in eight foreign countries. The candidates include five Asian nations and three Latin American ones: Cuba, Venezuela, and Nicaragua.[3] Negotiations are underway to allow port visits to each, and to open refueling sites there for Russian long-range aircraft.

Just one day later, in a throwback to Cold War military cooperation between the Soviet Union and client state Cuba, a Russian warship docked in Havana. As of yet, neither Moscow nor Havana has issued a formal explanation as to why the *Viktor Leonov*, a *Meridian*-class intelligence vessel, was dispatched to the Latin American state. However, the visit tracks with a growing Russian strategic footprint in the region.

Over the past several years, Moscow has devoted considerable diplomatic and political attention to the Americas. Consistent with its pursuit of a "multipolar" world and its efforts to reestablish itself as a great power, this engagement has prioritized contacts with ideological regimes which share a common anti-American worldview and similarly seek to dilute and counteract U.S. influence in the region.[4]

In Cuba, Russia has worked diligently over the past half-decade to rebuild its once-robust Cold War-era ties. This has entailed top level diplomatic visits by Russian officials to Havana (most prominent among them a November 2008 visit to the Cuban capital by then-Russian president Dmitry Medvedev), as well as new military agreements and revived cooperation on topics such as energy and nuclear cooperation.[5]

With Venezuela, Russia has succeeded in forging a robust military partnership, exploiting the radical ideology and expansionist tendencies of the Chavez regime in Caracas. Between 2001 and 2013, Venezuela is estimated to have purchased more than three-quarters of the $14.5 billion in arms sales carried out by Russia in the region.[6]

More recently, the Kremlin also has made concerted efforts to strengthen its relations with the Sandinista government of Daniel Ortega in Nicaragua. Since Ortega's return to power in

2007, Russia has emerged as a major investor in Nicaragua's military modernization, erecting a new military training facility in Managua and a munitions disposal plant outside of the Nicaraguan capital. Russia has also thrown open its warfare schools to the Ortega regime, with 25 Nicaraguan officers now reportedly being trained annually in Moscow.[7] The importance that Moscow attaches to this revitalized relationship was in evidence last spring, when Russia's General Staff Chief, Col. Gen. Valery Gerasimov, visited Managua on an official three-day visit[8]—an honor far outside the norm for a country of Nicaragua's modest military capabilities and political stature.

What drives Russian policy toward Latin America? Most recently, Moscow has focused on the region as part of stepped up efforts at international counter-narcotics cooperation. Pursuant to a March 2013 plan unveiled by the Kremlin's anti-drug czar, Viktor Ivanov, Russia is working to expand anti-drug operations with Latin American states.[9] This effort has already yielded notable results, among them a spring 2013 raid carried out in collaboration with Nicaragua that netted some 1.2 tons of cocaine and broke up a Central American gang linked to Mexico's notorious Los Zetas cartel.[10]

But Russia's interest in the Americas extends far beyond counter-narcotics. Moscow maintains significant economic equities in the region, although the volume of its trade (estimated at less than $14 billion annually[11]) is dwarfed by that of China. Nevertheless, Russia appears eager to position itself to exploit new economic opportunities, such as those that would result from the Nicaraguan government's ambitious plans to host a counterpart to the Panama Canal.[12] It may also be using compliant Latin American states to bolster its intelligence collection capabilities in the region, which are said to have grown significantly in recent years.

Russia's activities are strategic—and opportunistic. Although in practice Latin America remains far outside Russia's areas of core interest, the Russian government has clearly taken advantage of America's retraction from the region to improve its own position there in both economic and strategic terms.

Set against the backdrop of deteriorating U.S.-Russian bilateral relations writ large, this expanded presence should be cause for concern, in no small measure because of its overt military dimensions. Indeed, in his February 26th announcement, Russian Defense Minister Sergei Shoigu indicated that Moscow desires Latin American basing capabilities because of a need for refueling facilities near the equator.[13] This suggests that the Kremlin is now actively contemplating an expansion of its military activities in the Western Hemisphere, to include long-range missions by its combat aircraft.

IRAN'S INTRUSION

Although signs of Iran's presence in Latin America have been evident for some time, the U.S. government only truly became seized of the issue in the wake of a foiled October 2011 assassination attempt on Saudi Arabia's ambassador to the United States by elements of Iran's Revolutionary Guard Corps. The incident jolted official Washington awake to the very real threat Iran now poses south of the U.S. border.

This presence is not entirely new. Iran has exhibited some level of activity in the Americas since the 1980s, when its chief terrorist proxy, Hezbollah, became entrenched in the so-called "Triple Frontier" where Argentina, Brazil and Paraguay meet. But the Iranian regime's formal outreach to the region is significantly more recent, and largely an outgrowth of the warm personal relations between former Iranian president Mahmoud Ahmadinejad and late Venezuelan leader Hugo Chavez. These bonds—rooted in a shared revolutionary worldview—positioned the Chavez regime as a "gateway" into the region for the Islamic Republic, and facilitated Iran's efforts to build ties to other sympathetic regimes (most prominently those of Evo Morales in Bolivia and Rafael Correa in Ecuador).

Over the past decade, Iran's presence in Latin America has evolved along three main lines. First, Iran is engaging in outreach designed to build regional support for its nuclear effort and lessen the economic isolation it felt—at least until recently—as a result of U.S. and European sanctions. To this end, Iran has more than doubled its diplomatic presence in the region, and now boasts embassies in eleven Latin American countries.[14] In 2012, it also formally launched a Spanish-language public diplomacy vehicle known as *HispanTV*, which is intended to broaden the Islamic Republic's "ideological legitimacy" among Latin American audiences.[15] Iran is similarly estimated to have signed hundreds of trade and investment agreements with the countries of Latin America—although, with the notable exception of its contracts with Venezuela, most of these remain unrealized.

Second, Iran has sought to exploit Latin America as a hub for strategic resources. Best known in this regard are Iran's mining activities in the Roraima Basin that straddles the common border between Guyana and Venezuela, which are widely viewed as cover for the Iranian regime's extraction of uranium ore for use in its nuclear program.[16] Iran is similarly believed to have begun prospecting for uranium in multiple locations in Bolivia[17], and has signed a framework agreement to do the same in the future in Ecuador.[18] Iran is exploring the acquisition of other strategic minerals as well; it has become a formal "partner" in the development of Bolivia's reserves of lithium, which has applications for nuclear weapons development[19], and is known to be seeking at least two other minerals utilized in nuclear work and the production of ballistic missiles: tantalum and thorium.[20]

Third, Latin America has become an arena for Iranian asymmetric activity. The extent of Iran's reach were outlined most comprehensively by Argentine state prosecutor Alberto Nisman, whose May 2013 report detailed a continent-wide network of intelligence bases and logistical support centers spanning no fewer than eight countries.[21] Significantly, the Nisman report makes clear that, while these centers were instrumental in perpetrating the infamous 1994 AMIA bombing in Buenos Aires, they continue to remain operational today. Perhaps the most prominent manifestation of Iran's paramilitary presence, however, is the "regional defense school" of the left-wing Bolivarian Alliance for the Americas (ALBA) headquartered outside the city of Santa Cruz in eastern Bolivia. Construction of the facility was funded in part by the Iranian regime, which now reportedly plays a role in both the training and indoctrination of left-wing paramilitary elements at the institution.[22]

Iran's influence is being felt in the region in other ways as well. The Islamic Republic, for example, has launched notable grassroots proselytization efforts in a number of Latin American countries as part of its attempts to shore up support in the Americas.[23] Iran's domestic control methods, meanwhile, have become an export commodity. And the pro-government militias now brutally quelling opposition to the Maduro government in Venezuela bear more than a passing resemblance to Iran's feared *basij* domestic control units.[24]

In hindsight, the year 2012 can be said to have been the "high water" mark for Iran's presence in Latin America, and the Islamic Republic's activities have since receded in both scope and pace. But Iran should nonetheless be considered a significant strategic actor in the region, because along every prong of its outreach to the Americas, the Iranian regime is maintaining, if not expanding, its level of activity. Moreover, a number of political scenarios—among them Bolivia's recently-announced quest for a nuclear capability, Ecuador's attempts to ascend to the leadership of the ALBA bloc, and the controversial peace process now underway in Colombia—provide opportunities for Iran to preserve, and perhaps even expand, its regional influence in the years ahead.

CHINA'S ENTRENCHMENT

American attention to China's activities in Latin America dates back to 1997, when the Panamanian government granted the Hong Kong-based Hutchinson-Whampoa company a concession to administer the Panama Canal—a move that was broadly seen in Washington as a potential threat to U.S. national security, as well as an indicator of Beijing's growing designs on the Western Hemisphere. Since then, the U.S. government has watched while China has carried out what amounts to a dramatic expansion of its activities in Latin America.

In contrast to that of both Russia and Iran, China's footprint in the Americas is primarily economic in nature. Over the past several years, Chinese firms have established a significant "on the ground" presence in various economic sectors throughout Central and South America, including energy, mining, construction and telecommunications. In tandem, China's trade with countries of the region has increased exponentially, rising from $49 billion annually in 2004 to $260 billion a year in 2012.[25] This tracks with China's perception of the Americas as an attractive supply source for foodstuffs, as well as a lucrative destination for Chinese goods and a significant market for Chinese labor.[26]

This deepening economic activity has been mirrored by expanding political outreach. Then-Chinese President Hu Jintao's 2004 tour of the region launched an active schedule of official visits by top Chinese officials and policymakers to Latin American states (Cuba, Venezuela, Brazil, Mexico and Peru prominent among them). The number of concrete cooperation initiatives has ballooned as well; between the years 2000 and 2011, an estimated 121 bilateral agreements were signed between China and various countries in the region.[27] China has also increased its participation in assorted Latin American regional organizations, joining the Organization of American States as a "permanent observer" in 2004 and becoming a "donor member" of the Inter-American Development Bank in 2008.

Militarily, meanwhile, China has pursued a multi-faceted strategy designed to maximize its contacts with, and influence among, Latin American states. Experts have identified five distinct dimensions of this outreach: humanitarian assistance, peacekeeping, military exchanges, arms sales, and technology transfer.[28] Through its efforts on these fronts, Beijing has secured Bolivia, Venezuela and Ecuador as arms clients, and significantly bolstered its interaction with regional militaries through personnel exchanges, joint maneuvers and cooperative trainings.

These public activities have been matched by more quiet—and questionable—ones. For example, China has become a contributor to Argentina's nuclear program, despite the growing insolvency of the government of Cristina Fernandez de Kirchner in Buenos Aires.[29] It has assisted both Venezuela and Bolivia in the development and launch of surveillance satellites.[30] And it has committed, by proxy, to the construction of a massive 50-mile passageway for maritime transit between the Pacific and Atlantic in Nicaragua, despite the astronomical projected price-tag (an estimated $40 billion).[31] These initiatives, and others, suggest that Beijing sees the region at least in part as an arena for strategic competition, and one where the PRC has the ability to significantly improve its geopolitical position.

All of the initiatives above are consistent with China's larger foreign policy vision. Since the late 1990s, Beijing has pursued a "going out" policy, which has been described as "a strategy designed to systematically promote exports, gain access to needed resources, and accelerate the development of its multilateral enterprises."[32] Latin America fits squarely into this initiative as both a marketplace and a venue for Chinese soft power, to the point where China and Latin America have become "essential economic partners."[33] China's engagement in the Western Hemisphere likewise tracks with its long-standing desire for a "multipolar world" in which America's perceived hegemony in international affairs is diminished. These rationales go a long way toward explaining why China's relations with the region remain largely unaltered, despite a year of tremendous political change in the Americas following the death of Hugo Chavez, and a significant domestic transition in China with the ascension of Xi Jinping to the presidency of the PRC.

Beijing's interest in the Americas, moreover, likely will be bolstered further in the years ahead by two trends. The first is an increasingly active, interventionist Chinese foreign policy, which is now on display in the Middle East, Africa, and in China's own territorial backyard of the Asia-Pacific. The second is a perception now prevalent in Beijing that

America is receding politically from the world stage, including in its own hemisphere, thereby leaving a void that China now has greater opportunity to fill.

MONROE... AND AFTER

In 1823, in his seventh State of the Union address, President James Monroe warned the nations of Europe against intervention in the newly-independent countries of Latin America, whose political independence America would henceforth preserve and protect. That statement, which came to be known as the "Monroe Doctrine," became a lasting guidepost for U.S. policy toward the Americas.

Until now. Last Fall, in a speech before the Organization of the American States, Secretary of State John Kerry announced with great fanfare that the "era of the Monroe Doctrine is over."[34] Kerry's pronouncement was intended to reassure regional powers that the heavy-handed interventionism that at times had characterized America's approach to the region was a thing of the past. But it also served notice to foreign powers that the United States has no plans to contest or compete with their growing influence south of our border.

This represents a dangerous signal. Through their engagement in Latin America, Russia, Iran, and China are already having a profound effect upon the complexion of the region, and doing so in ways that are deeply detrimental to the United States. The resulting costs to American security and U.S. economic interests must be weighed against any potential benefits or savings from the Administration's current minimalist policy toward the region.

ENDNOTES:

[1] James Clapper, Testimony before the Senate Select Committee on Intelligence, January 29, 2014, http://www.intelligence.senate.gov/140129/clapper.pdf.

[2] See J.D. Gordon, "The Decline of U.S. Influence in Latin America," AFPC *Defense Dossier* iss. 9, December 2013, http://www.afpc.org/files/december2013.pdf.

[3] "Russia Seeks Several Military Bases Abroad – Defense Minister," RIA Novosti (Moscow), February 26, 2014, http://en.ria.ru/military_news/20140226/187917901/Russia-Seeks-Several-Military-Bases-Abroad--Defense-Minister.html.

[4] Stephen Blank, "Russia in Latin America: Geopolitical Games in the US's Neighborhood," IFRI *Russie.Nie.Visions* no. 38, April 2009, http://www.ifri.org/?page=contribution-detail&id=5332&id_provenance=97.

[5] Marc Frank, "Moscow Seeks to Mend Cuba Ties," *Financial Times*, December 1, 2008, http://www.ft.com/intl/cms/s/0/9b22dd90-bf49-11dd-ae63-0000779fd18c.html#axzz2wTKqc6l4; "Russia, Cuba Agree to Renew Joint Nuclear Research," RIA Novosti (Moscow), May 27, 2009, http://en.ria.ru/russia/20090527/155104039.html.

[6] Alejandro Hinds, "Venezuela compro 76% de las Armas que Rusia Vendio a America Latina," *El Nacional* (Caracas), May 14, 2013, http://www.el-nacional.com/mundo/armas-compra-rosoboronexport-rusia-sipri-venezuela_0_189581219.html.

[7] Author's interviews, Managua, Nicaragua, June 2013.

[8] "Top Russian Military Brass Visits Nicaragua," *Nicaragua Dispatch*, April 22, 2013, http://nicaraguadispatch.com/2013/04/top-russian-military-brass-visits-nicaragua/7413/.

[9] See, for example, James Bargent, "Russia Looks to Increase Influence in Latin American Drug War," *InsightCrime*, March 20, 2013, http://www.insightcrime.org/news-briefs/russia-influence-latin-america-drug-war.

[10] "Russia & Nicaragua Bust Zeta-Linked Drug Ring in Joint Operation," *Fox News Latino*, March 13, 2013, http://latino.foxnews.com/latino/news/2013/03/13/russia-nicaragua-bust-zeta-linked-drug-ring-in-joint-operation/.

[11] International Monetary Fund, Directorate of Trade Statistics, "Annual figures for 2012," September 2013.

[12] Jonathan Watts, "Nicaragua Gives Chinese Firm Contract to Build Alternative to Panama Canal," *Guardian* (London), June 6, 2013, http://www.theguardian.com/world/2013/jun/06/nicaragua-china-panama-canal.

[13] Bill Vourvoulias, "Russia Reportedly Eyeing Latin America as Part of Overseas Military Base Expansion," *Fox News Latino*, March 4, 2014, http://latino.foxnews.com/latino/news/2014/03/04/russia-reportedly-eyeing-latin-america-as-part-overseas-military-base-expansion/.

[14] These countries are Argentina, Bolivia, Brazil, Chile, Colombia, Cuba, Ecuador, Mexico, Nicaragua, Uruguay and Venezuela.

[15] Ian Black, "Iran to Launch Spanish-Language Television Channel," *Guardian* (London), September 30, 2010, http://www.guardian.co.uk/world/2010/sep/30/iran-spanish-language-television; "Iran Launches Spanish TV Channel," Associated Press, January 31, 2012, http://www.guardian.co.uk/world/2012/jan/31/iran-launches-spanish-tv-channel.

[16] See, for example, Stephen Johnson, *Iran's Influence in the Americas* (Washington, DC: Center for Strategic & International Studies, March 2012), xiv, http://csis.org/files/publication/120312_Johnson_Iran%27sInfluence_web.pdf.

[17] Author's interviews, La Paz and Santa Cruz, Bolivia, January-February 2012.

[18] See Jose Cardenas, "Iran's Man in Ecuador," *Foreign Policy*, February 15, 2011, http://shadow.foreignpolicy.com/posts/2011/02/15/irans_man_in_ecuador.

[19] "Iran 'Partner' in the Industrialization of Bolivia's Lithium Reserves," *MercoPress*, October 30, 2010, http://en.mercopress.com/2010/10/30/iran-partner-in-the-industrialization-of-bolivia-s-lithium-reserves.

[20] Author's interviews in Chile, Bolivia and Argentina, January-February 2012.

[21] The English-language translation of the indictment is available online at http://www.defenddemocracy.org/stuff/uploads/documents/summary_%2831_pages%29.pdf.

[22] See, for example, Jon B. Purdue, *The War of All the People: The Nexus of Latin American Radicalism and Middle Eastern Terrorism* (Dulles, VA: Potomac Books, 2012), 154-156.

[23] See, for example, Joby Warrick, "With Lure of Religious Classes, Iran Seeks to Recruit Latin Americans," *Washington Post*, August 10, 2013, http://www.washingtonpost.com/world/national-security/with-lure-of-religion-classes-iran-seeks-to-recruit-latin-americans/2013/08/10/8c3592c6-f626-11e2-9434-60440856fadf_story.html.

[24] Joseph Humire, "Iran Propping up Venezuela's Repressive Militias," *Washington Times*, March 18, 2014, http://www.washingtontimes.com/news/2014/mar/17/humire-irans-basij-props-up-venezuelas-repressive-/.

[25] *Direction of Trade Statistics Yearbook* (Washington, DC: International Monetary Fund, 2012), 924; International Monetary Fund, Directorate of Trade Statistics, "Annual figures for 2012," September 2013.

[26] R. Evan Ellis, "Russia, Iran and China in Latin America: Evaluating the Threat," *AFPC Defense Dossier* iss. 9, December 2013, http://www.afpc.org/files/december2013.pdf.

[27] Katherine Koleski, "Backgrounder: China in Latin America," U.S.-China Economic & Security Review Commission, May 27, 2011, http://origin.www.uscc.gov/sites/default/files/Research/Backgrounder_China_in_Latin_America.pdf.

[28] Gabriel Marcella, "China's Military Activity in Latin America," *Americas Quarterly*, Winter 2012, http://www.americasquarterly.org/Marcella.

[29] See, for example, "China Offers Argentina Nuclear Power Technology," July 14, 2010, http://www.laht.com/article.asp?ArticleId=360370&CategoryId=14093.

[30] "China Delivers Control of Satellite to Venezuela," Xinhua (Beijing), September 3, 2013, http://news.xinhuanet.com/english/china/2013-09/03/c_132687197.htm; "China Launches Communications Satellite for Bolivia," Xinhua (Beijing), December 21, 2013, http://www.spacedaily.com/reports/China_launches_communications_satellite_for_Bolivia_999.html.

[31] See Eric Hannis, "Building a Canal to Power," *U.S. News & World Report*, October 22, 2013, http://www.usnews.com/opinion/blogs/world-report/2013/10/22/china-challenges-american-primacy-in-central-america-with-nicaraguan-canal.

[32] Peter Hakim and Margaret Myers, "China and Latin America in 2013," *China Policy Review*, January 9, 2014, http://www.thedialogue.org/page.cfm?pageID=32&pubID=3491.

[33] Ibid.

[34] Keith Johnson, "Kerry Makes It Official: 'Era of Monroe Doctrine is Over,'" *Wall Street Journal*, November 18, 2013, http://blogs.wsj.com/washwire/2013/11/18/kerry-makes-it-official-era-of-monroe-doctrine-is-over/.

Mr. SALMON. Thank you, Mr. Berman.

Mr. Claver-Carone.

STATEMENT OF MR. MAURICIO CLAVER–CARONE, EXECUTIVE DIRECTOR, CUBA DEMOCRACY ADVOCATES

Mr. CLAVER-CARONE. Thank you, Mr. Chairman, Ranking Member, members of the subcommittee.

It is really a privilege to be here today to discuss this important and consequential issue regarding Latin America which directly affects the national interest of the United States.

My testimony can be summarized as follows: The Cuban dictatorship is working systematically against democratic institutions in Latin America. Autocracies like Cuba's work systematically using subterfuge, coercion, censorship, and state-sponsored violence including lethal force and terrorism.

Thus, the regions democracies, led by the United States, must also work systematically to protect and promote its democratic institutions, and democracies work systematically by holding human rights violators accountable, giving voice, legal assistance and protection to the victims, economic sanctions and diplomatic pressure and by promoting successful evidence-based aid programs to break the cycle of poverty and instability, and obviously that is an issue for another hearing.

Allow me to elaborate a bit on this. In the 1980s, it was commonly stated that the road to freedom in Havana runs through Managua, alluding to a cause-effect from an end to the Cuban-backed Sandinista dictatorship of Daniel Ortega in Nicaragua. In the last decade, this statement has morphed into the road to freedom in Havana runs through Caracas, referring to the Cuban-backed Bolivarian Governments of the late Hugo Chávez and Nicolás Maduro in Venezuela.

Undoubtedly, both roads represent noble and important goals albeit temporary short-term solutions, the reason being that the Sandinista Government of the 1980s and the Bolivarian Government of today are symptoms, not remedies, of a greater illness.

The fact remains that no nation in Latin America will enjoy the long-term benefits of freedom, democracy and security so long as the dictatorship of the Castro brothers remains in power in Havana.

As such, a more accurate statement would be the road to long-term freedom, democracy and security in Latin America runs through Havana. The Castro regime remains as resolute today to subvert democratic institutions, to direct and sponsor violent agitators and support autocrats throughout the region and the world as it did in the '60s, '70s and '80s.

Granted, its tactics and scope have been diminished, mostly due to the economic realities stemming from the end of massive Soviet subsidies through 1991, but its antagonistic aims are unwavering.

No wishful thinking or accommodation policy, which I believe are interchangeable, will make this go away. Moreover, to underestimate the skill, diligence and effectiveness of Cuba's intelligence and security forces is a grave mistake, the proportions of which we are witnessing today in Venezuela.

After all, the erosion of Venezuela's democratic institutions and its government's repressive practices are the result of a protracted systematic effort spanning over a decade of penetration and control by the Cuban dictatorship, and Ambassador Reich mentioned what Luis Miquilena, a former mentor to Hugo Chávez, said.

Thus, it should be a priority for all democracies in Latin America, led by the United States, to support the democratic forces in Cuba working to end the dictatorship of the Castro brothers. That is the remedy.

Unfortunately, that has not been the case and last month Latin America's democratically-elected leaders paraded through Havana for a summit of the CELAC, which is an anti-U.S. concoction of Hugo Chávez.

Currently, the organization's rotating presidency is, ironically, held by General Raul Castro. Similarly, these elected leaders were not interested nor concerned that Cuba's regime had threatened, beaten and arrested hundreds of the island's democracy advocates who had tried to plan and hold a parallel summit to discuss the lack of freedom and human rights in Cuba.

This trend is reversible, but the leadership of the United States is vital. Undoubtedly, the democracies of Latin America need to step up to their own responsibilities, but in the cost benefit analysis that all political leaders make, they need to be left with no doubt that the benefits of standing up for freedom and democracy in Cuba outweigh the cost.

Whether we like it or not, only the United States can tip that balance, hence, the title of today's hearing. To be clear, United States is not the cause of Latin America's problems.

To the contrary, it represents the solution. U.S. leadership in the region should be public, unquestionable and unwavering, particularly in regards to shared values of freedom, democracy and security.

Our democratic allies in the region should know and anticipate the benefits derived from embracing and promoting democratic practices, and likewise, autocrats should know and anticipate the consequences of undemocratic practices and illegal acts.

Unfortunately, currently neither is the case. We are witnessing the first with Venezuela. The silence of Latin America's leaders amid the violent suppression of dissent by the government of Nicolás Maduro is scandalous. The reasons for their silence amid the arrest, torture and murder of Venezuelan students is similar to the rationale for embracing the Castro dictatorship by the CELAC summit in Havana—how instead of leading and encouraging the region's democrats and holding Maduro's government accountable, the United States is unwittingly, and I don't think it is purposefully, contributing to their silence.

For example, this past Friday the Panamanian Government ceded its seat at the Organization of American States to Venezuelan legislator María Corina Machado, a leading opposition figure, to renounce the human rights abuses of the Maduro government.

I remind you in 1988–89 Venezuela's democratic government had supported Panama's democratic opposition and did the same for them, thus Panama's democrats remain grateful.

The U.S. should have applauded this gesture by Panama and it did so after the fact but, unfortunately, the United States initially sought to dissuade the Panamanian Government from accrediting María Corina Machado to speak at the OAS. That is a lamentable fact and I would urge the subcommittee to ask the State Department for its rationale.

In the interest of time, the U.S. should also be making the benefits of supporting Venezuela's democratic institutions absolutely clear and not muddying the message.

In the same vein, the consequences for undemocratic practices and illegal acts should be absolutely clear and there is no better opportunity to do so than regarding the Castro regime's recent smuggling of weapons to North Korea in blatant violation of international law.

As you know, in July 2013 the North Korean flag vessel, Chong Chon Gang, was intercepted with weaponry hidden under 200,000 bags of sugar. This month, the U.N.'s panel of experts released its official report on North Korea's illegal trafficking of weapons in conjunction with Castro's regime.

The panel concluded that both the shipment in itself and the transaction between Cuba and North Korea were international sanctions violations. Let me emphasize this shipment constituted the largest amount of arms and related material interdicted to or from North Korea since the adoption of the U.N. Security Council's resolution, and as for Cuba, it is the first time a nation in the Western Hemisphere was found in violation of U.N. sanctions.

The report noted similar patterns by other North Korean ships. Thus, similar ships have simply gotten away, and such egregious practices should not be inconsequential. Thus far, it would send a demoralizing message to Panama, which put up its resources and reputation, and but moreover, it would show that inaction breeds impunity.

And as my time is over, I would just finally state a third factor, it is essential that the United States lead, and once again it all goes back to leadership, of the region's defense, promotion and application of the Inter-American Democratic Charter.

Otherwise, it will become irrelevant and no other nation in the hemisphere will do that.

[The prepared statement of Mr. Claver-Carone follows:]

MAURICIO CLAVER-CARONE

EXECUTIVE DIRECTOR, CUBA DEMOCRACY ADVOCATES

HOUSE COMMITTEE ON FOREIGN AFFAIRS

Tuesday, March 25, 2014

"U.S. Disengagement from Latin America: Compromised Security and Economic Interests"

Thank you, Mr. Chairman, Ranking Member and Members of the Committee.

It's truly a privilege to join you here today to discuss this important and consequential issue regarding Latin America, which directly affects the national interests of the United States.

My name is Mauricio Claver-Carone and I'm the Executive Director of Cuba Democracy Advocates, a non-profit, non-partisan organization dedicated to the promotion of human rights, democracy and the rule of law in Cuba.

My testimony can be summarized as follows:

The Cuban dictatorship is working systematically against democratic institutions in Latin America.

Autocracies, such as Cuba's, work systematically using subterfuge, coercion, censorship and state-sponsored violence, including lethal force and terrorism.

Thus, the region's democrats -- led by the United States -- must also work systematically to protect and promote its democratic institutions.

Democracies work systematically by holding human rights violators accountable; giving voice, legal assistance and protection to the victims; economic sanctions and diplomatic pressure; and by promoting successful evidence-based aid programs to break the cycle of poverty and instability.

Allow me to elaborate:

In the 1980s, it was commonly stated that: "*The road to freedom in Havana runs through Managua,*" alluding to a cause-effect from an end to the Cuban-backed Sandinista dictatorship of Daniel Ortega in Nicaragua.

In the last decade, this statement morphed into: "*The road to freedom in Havana runs through Caracas,*" referring to the Cuban-backed Bolivarian governments of the late Hugo Chavez and Nicolas Maduro in Venezuela.

Undoubtedly, both roads represent noble and important goals, albeit temporary, short-term solutions. The reason being that the Sandinista government of the 1980s and the Bolivarian governments of today are symptoms -- not remedies -- of a greater illness.

The fact remains that no nation in Latin America will enjoy the long-term benefits of freedom, democracy and security, so long as the dictatorship of the Castro brothers remains in power in Havana.

As such, a more accurate statement would be: *"The road to long-term freedom, democracy and security in Latin America runs through Havana."*

The Castro regime remains as resolute today to subvert democratic institutions, direct and sponsor violent agitators and support autocrats throughout the region -- and the world -- as it did in the 1960s, 1970s and 1980s. Granted, its tactics and scope have been diminished, mostly due to the economic realities stemming from the end of massive Soviet subsidies through 1991, but its antagonistic aims are unwavering.

No wishful thinking or accommodation policy -- both interchangeable -- will make this go away. Moreover, to underestimate the skill, diligence and effectiveness of Cuba's intelligence and security forces is a grave mistake -- the proportions of which we are witnessing today in Venezuela.

After all, the erosion of Venezuela's democratic institutions and its government's repressive practices, are the result of a protracted, systematic effort -- spanning over a decade -- of penetration and control by the Cuban dictatorship.

As Luis Miquilena, former Venezuelan Minister of the Interior, head of its National Assembly and mentor to Hugo Chavez, recently repented in an interview:

"Venezuela today is a country that is practically occupied by the henchmen of two international criminals, Cuba's Castro brothers. They have introduced in Venezuela a true army of occupation. The Cubans run the maritime ports, airports, communications, the most essential issues in Venezuela. We are in the hands of a foreign country."

Thus, it should be a priority for all democrats in Latin America -- led by the United States -- to support the democratic forces in Cuba working to end the dictatorship of the Castro brothers. That is the remedy.

Unfortunately, that has not been the case.

Last month, Latin America's democratically elected leaders paraded through Havana for a summit of the Community of Latin American States ("CELAC," in Spanish), an anti-U.S. concoction of Hugo Chavez. Currently, the organization's rotating presidency is held by General Raul Castro.

Seemingly these elected leaders were neither interested nor concerned that Cuba's regime had threatened, beaten and arrested hundreds of the island's democracy advocates who had tried to plan and hold a parallel summit to discuss the lack of freedom and human rights in Cuba.

Why would Latin America's democratically elected leaders willingly participate in such a hypocritical charade? What does Cuba's regime offer them that they would stake the loss of credibility by attending?

Some take part in these charades because they fear radical agitators back home. That is the case of Mexico's President Enrique Peña Nieto. Pulitzer Prize-winning journalist Andres Oppenheimer was recently in Mexico, where he interviewed various well-placed insiders, and wrote: "*President Enrique Peña Nieto's disregard for the defense of universal rights and basic freedoms in Cuba and Venezuela is partly due to fear that these two countries could use their clout with Mexico's leftist movements to stir up trouble at home.*"

Others attend to pursue business deals without transparency. Such is the case of Brazil's President Dilma Rousseff. During the CELAC summit, Rousseff joined Castro for the official inauguration of the newly-expanded Port of Mariel, a collaboration of the Brazilian conglomerate Odebrecht Group and the Cuban military. This was the same facility from which Cuba's recent smuggling of illegal weapons to North Korea originated. In an unprecedented move, the Brazilian government has now "classified" all documents related to the Odebrecht-Cuban military venture.

Lastly, others lack democratic zeal and conviction. These are the leaders who harbor authoritarian ambitions that the Cuban regime is helping them achieve. We'll return to them at the conclusion.

This trend is reversible -- but the leadership of the United States is vital.

Undoubtedly, the democrats of Latin America need to step up to their own responsibilities, but in the cost-benefit analysis that all political leaders make, they need to be left with no doubt that the benefits of standing up for freedom and democracy in Cuba outweigh the costs. Whether we like it or not, only the United States can tip that balance.

Hence the title of today's hearing, "U.S. Disengagement from Latin America: Compromised Security and Economic Interests."

To be clear, the United States is not the cause of Latin America's problems. To the contrary, it represents the solution. U.S. leadership in the region should be public, unquestionable and unwavering, particularly as regards the shared values of freedom, democracy and security.

Our democratic allies in the region should know and anticipate the benefits derived from embracing and promoting democratic practices. Likewise, autocrats should know and anticipate the consequences of undemocratic practices and illegal acts.

Currently, neither is the case.

We are witnessing the first with Venezuela. The silence of Latin America's leaders amid the violent suppression of dissent by the government of Nicolas Maduro is scandalous.

The reasons for their silence, amid the arrest, torture and murder of Venezuelan students, is similar to their rationale for embracing the Castro dictatorship at the CELAC summit in Havana, while Cuban democracy activists were being beaten and arrested there.

However, instead of leading and encouraging the region's democrats in holding Maduro's government accountable, the United States is -- unwittingly -- contributing to their silence.

For example, this past Friday, the Panamanian government ceded its seat at the Organization of American States ("OAS") to Venezuelan legislator Maria Corina Machado, a leading opposition figure, to denounce the human rights abuses of the Maduro government.

In 1988-1989, Venezuela's democratic government had supported Panama's democratic opposition against the repression of Manuel Noriega's regime, including their right to be heard at the OAS. Thus, Panama's democrats remain grateful.

The U.S. should have applauded this gesture by Panama. Yet, unfortunately, the United States initially sought to dissuade the Panamanian government from accrediting Maria Corina Machado to speak at the OAS.

That is a lamentable fact. I would urge the Committee to ask the U.S. Department of State for its rationale.

A democratic nation in Latin America gives a voice, a platform, to one of the leading democratic figures that Nicolas Maduro is forcefully trying to silence -- even threatening her with imprisonment -- and the U.S. grimaces.

What message does that send to the rest of Latin America's democrats? Why should they then speak out? Who's going to support them when Cuba's regime and its agitators take reprisals? What message does this send to Venezuela's courageous democracy activists?

The U.S. should be making the benefits of supporting Venezuela's democratic institutions absolutely clear -- not muddying the message.

In the same vein, the consequences for undemocratic practices and illegal acts should be absolutely clear.

There is no better opportunity to do so than regarding the Castro regime's recent smuggling of weapons to North Korea, in blatant violation of international law.

In July 2013, a North Korean flagged vessel, Chong Chon Gang, was intercepted by Panama carrying weaponry from Cuba hidden under 200,000 bags of sugar.

This month, the U.N.'s Panel of Experts ("Panel") released its official report on North Korea's illegal trafficking of weapons, in conjunction with Cuba's Castro regime.

The Panel concluded that both the shipment itself and the transaction between Cuba and North Korea were international sanctions violations.

This shipment constituted the largest amount of arms and related materiel interdicted to or from North Korea since the adoption of U.N. Security Council Resolution 1718 (2006).

As for Cuba, it's the first time a nation in the Western Hemisphere is found in violation of U.N. sanctions.

The report noted similar Cuba trafficking patterns by other North Korean ships in the recent past. In other words, it's believed similar shipments have gotten away.

To understand the magnitude of this shipment, Scott Snyder, a Korea expert at the Council of Foreign Relations, explained:

"If the North Korean-flagged Chong Chon Gang had been successful in bringing its MiG-21 cargo to North Korea, the transaction with Cuba might have been the biggest sale of fighter plane related equipment since a MiG sale from Kazakhstan in 1999. The Chong Chon Gang cargo included mint-condition rocket propelled grenades (RPGs) that are essential to North Korea's efforts to extend its conventional reach on the peninsula as USFK (United States Forces Korea) command elements transition south from Seoul to Pyeongtaek."

Such egregious practices should not be inconsequential.

Otherwise, it would send a demoralizing message to our democratic ally, Panama, which put its resources and reputation on the line to intercept the vessel. Other democratic nations wouldn't find it worth the cost and energy of pursuing similar violations in the future.

Moreover, inaction breeds impunity. If Cuba's regime does not face any consequences, it would embolden non-democratic actors in Venezuela and other nations to do the same. There has long been suspicion that Venezuela and Ecuador have been helping Iran and Syria skirt the U.S.'s financial sanctions. Russia is currently seeking to establish military bases in the region. They would surely interpret any inaction as a green-light.

One immediate consequence the United States should adopt is to prohibit transactions with Cuba's military conglomerate, GAESA, run by Raul Castro's son-in-law, General Luis Alberto Rodriguez Lopez-Callejas. GAESA, which controls over 80% of Cuba's economy, was at the center of the transactions linked to the North Korea arms smuggling operation.

Currently, every single U.S. "people-to-people" traveler that visits Cuba stays at one of GAESA's 4 and 5 star hotels and resorts. Tourism represents GAESA's most lucrative enterprise. Such transactions should be prohibited.

Finally, it's essential that the United States lead the region's defense, promotion and application of the Inter-American Democratic Charter ("Charter"). Otherwise, it will become irrelevant.

The authoritarian ambitions of Venezuela's Nicolas Maduro, Ecuador's Rafael Correa, Bolivia's Evo Morales, Argentina's Cristina Fernandez de Kirchner and Nicaragua's Daniel Ortega are no secret.

What has inhibited them -- thus far -- is the institutionalization of representative democracy as the backbone of hemispheric relations, as was agreed upon in the 2001 Inter-American Democratic Charter signed by 34 of the 35 countries of the Western Hemisphere. To skirt the Charter, they try to manipulate laws and institutions and exert greater executive control while maintaining a facade of democracy.

The biggest deterrent to breaking their public commitments to representative democracy has been the omnipresent economic isolation of Cuba as the result of U.S. sanctions. These leaders are keenly aware that they need the United States to survive economically. For example, Venezuela is entirely dependent on exporting oil to -- and importing gas from -- the United States. Thus U.S. sanctions on Cuba serve as "the stick" to "the carrot" of the Inter-American Democratic Charter and obeisance, if not enforcement, of its principles.

It's precisely the authoritarian underbelly of these Latin American leaders that makes them such zealous lobbyists for the end of U.S. sanctions on Cuba. It's for this reason that they want to see the Castro regime embraced despite its blatant disregard for representative democracy. Such a U.S. policy change would allow them to accelerate their own authoritarian tendencies and free their zeal for absolute power.

If U.S. sanctions toward Cuba are lifted and Castro's dictatorship is embraced -- what's to keep a return to the Latin American dictatorships of the 20th Century?

The people of the Americas can't afford a return to the dictatorships -- whether of the left or the right -- that once ruled Latin America. It would severely damage the 21st century national interests of the United States.

Sadly, plenty of Latin American "leaders" would gladly seize the opportunity to permanently close the door on democracy.

Let's not hand them the opportunity.

Mr. Chairman, this concludes my testimony. Again, I truly appreciate the invitation and the opportunity to speak before you and the Committee. I will be pleased to respond to any questions.

Mr. SALMON. Thank you.
Mr. Shifter.

STATEMENT OF MR. MICHAEL SHIFTER, PRESIDENT, INTER-AMERICAN DIALOGUE

Mr. SHIFTER. Thank you very much, Mr. Chairman, Ranking Member Sires, other members of the subcommittee. I appreciate this opportunity to appear before you today to talk about U.S. policy toward Latin America.

The U.S. relationship with Latin America has changed in fundamental ways in recent years and has become more distant, more so in South America than in Mexico and Central America.

The reasons for this are deep and many and cannot be traced to any single administration or policy. The main explanation is, ironically, Latin America's economic, social, even political progress over the last decade.

The region is more politically confident and independent on the world stage. It continues to expand its global ties. The United States too has changed over the same period. The 2008 financial crisis hit hard.

We have endured two draining wars. Our highest-level officials have been distracted elsewhere. The presence of non-hemispheric actors in Latin America has grown. In the era of globalization, this is natural.

China is involved through trade, financing and, to a lesser extent, investment. Of greater concern are the roles of Russia and Iran. Over the past dozen years, Russia has sold arms to the region at an estimated $14.5 billion—it has been said over three-quarters of that to Venezuela.

The recent statement by Russia's defense minister about intentions to increase their presence in Venezuela, Nicaragua and Cuba was probably mostly posturing for domestic political consumption, but especially given what is happening today in Ukraine they need to be followed very closely and very carefully.

Iran's activities too should be carefully monitored. There is ample information about money laundering operations. But so far, there has been no credible proof of threats posed by Iran-linked groups.

The Obama administration, in my judgment, has been vigilant about these questions and needs to marshal resources to follow what is happening as closely as possible in the region. At the same time, there is little indication today that such actors pose a serious danger or threat to U.S. interests.

There is great concern about Venezuela as well there should be. Even minimal human rights and democratic safeguards have eroded. The government's repression of protestors, persecution of political opponents and restrictions on press freedom are even worse than during the Chávez era.

In such a polarized country, anything can happen. Venezuela shows how difficult it is for the United States to exercise leadership in the current environment. During the Chávez years, Venezuela gained allies through lavish spending. The intent was to curtail the influence of the United States in this hemisphere.

Fortunately, ALBA, the anti-U.S. group that Chávez created and led, has become weaker even before Chávez's death in March of last year. The deep economic and continuing crisis in Venezuela has hurt ALBA's capacity to act throughout the region.

Unfortunately, however, at a regional level where there is so much polarization and fragmentation, there has not been much will to act regarding Venezuela. The OAS has all the instruments at its disposal to apply pressure but unfortunately the will isn't there for both economic and for political reasons.

The Venezuelan crisis shows how critical it is for the United States to become more engaged than it has been in regional affairs. It can do this in several ways.

The United States cannot, unfortunately, act alone. It needs to act in concert with others. I do believe that the United States should be more involved in the OAS, not just saying what the OAS needs to do but actually coming up with ideas, proposals and reforms and mobilizing support and allies around those proposals.

The U.S. efforts on strengthening human rights have been commendable but there has been no energy and no hard work, as far as I can tell, on the political side. The U.S. has been withdrawn and disengaged. The effort has not been made.

The second way is to deepen our relationship with Brazil. This is very difficult in the short term—we all realize that. But U.S. policy will be limited in this hemisphere, in this region, unless there is sustained focus on relations with the region's preeminent economic power.

Third, strengthen relations with Mexico, Colombia, Peru and Chile. The administration is doing this, to its credit, but especially with Mexico it is hard to make progress without immigration reform and progress on other items on the domestic agenda in the United States.

The failure to do this hurts our efforts to reengage with Mexico and also with other countries in Latin America. And finally, we cannot reduce our engagement and cooperation on Latin American security issues.

These need to be sustained not only in Central America and Mexico but even in Colombia, which has been a success story for U.S. policy in this hemisphere that we should not forget. But we need to continue to invest with a strategic ally that reflects our commitment to the region.

Thank you very much.

[The prepared statement of Mr. Shifter follows:]

Statement of Michael Shifter
President, Inter-American Dialogue
Committee on Foreign Affairs
Subcommittee on the Western Hemisphere
"U.S. Disengagement from Latin America: Compromised Security and Economic
Interests"
March 25, 2014

Chairman Salmon, Ranking Member Sires, and members of the Subcommittee on the Western Hemisphere, I very much appreciate the opportunity to appear before you today to share my views about US policy towards Latin America. I commend the Committee for holding this important and timely hearing.

Today there is, for good reason, great concern about the situation in Venezuela. The scenario that many of us had warned of and feared these past dozen years – a surge in violence and dramatic deterioration of the already minimal human rights and democratic safeguards – has unfortunately come to pass. The outlook is ominous. No one knows with certainty how far the Venezuela government is prepared to go in using repressive tactics against peaceful protesters, persecuting political opponents, and restricting press freedom. Since mid-February, violence in Venezuela has claimed more than 30 lives. In such a polarized society, with high levels of mistrust and rancor, anything can happen.

Washington's inability to measurably influence the unfolding tragedy in Venezuela has given a renewed rise to questioning about the US's role and presence in Latin America. The concern is valid. But merely criticizing the current administration for being disengaged and indifferent to what is happening in the region is somewhat misplaced.

Rather than blame the current or previous US administrations, it is best to put today's situation in proper perspective. The fact is over the past decade or so, Latin America has changed in profound ways. Many Latin American economies have performed well and have multiplied their global ties. Politically, they are increasingly confident on the world stage. More than in the recent past, the United States is now but one of many countries involved in the region's affairs.

The United States, too, has changed over the same period. The 2008 financial crisis hit hard and exposed weaknesses in our management of fiscal affairs. The US has endured two draining wars. Senior officials have, understandably, been distracted from this hemisphere. These and other problems – including widening inequality (while the income gap has narrowed in many Latin American countries) and the inability of our political system to reach consensus and effectively address significant national challenges – have not gone unnoticed by our neighbors to the South.

The result is that the US relationship with Latin America – which, to be sure, varies widely from country to country – has in general become more distant. The US and Latin America have been moving in separate ways. The drift is a long-term trend -- the direct consequence of globalization and, to a large extent, economic and political progress in Latin America. Particular US policies may have helped alter this tendency to a certain degree -- on the margins -- but the basic direction in this hemisphere has been clear for some time.[1]

It is also too simplistic to say that, in the past, the United States was warmly embraced in Latin America, whereas today it has lost influence and is not taken seriously. The truth is more complicated. The United States has long been viewed with suspicion and resentment by certain sectors of Latin American societies. Vice President Richard Nixon's violent reception during his 1958 visit to Venezuela, then an important US ally, illustrates the point.

At the same time, the absence of US engagement and influence in the region today is often exaggerated. A close examination of increased trade and investment in a number of Latin American countries reflects a US private sector that has moved to take advantage of attractive opportunities with our southern neighbors.[2] The US has free trade agreements with 11 Latin American countries. If the Trans-Pacific Partnership comes to fruition, that would mean even closer commercial ties with several countries in Latin America.

On the security front, US cooperation with Colombia and Peru has produced real benefits over a sustained period of time. Other security policies in Mexico and Central America -- while inadequate and sometimes misguided -- have, on balance, yielded some useful results. Although the United States has made modest progress on a new agenda focused on energy, education, science, and technology, there is some promise for more significant advance in coming years.

It is also a mistake to believe that the creation of regional organizations that do not include the United States (or Canada) is something new that should be viewed as threatening to US interests. The reality is that shared cultural heritage and affinities account for a strong strand of regionalism and integration that far predates the recently established organizations of UNASUR and CELAC. Moreover, the effectiveness of these organizations remains to be seen.

One core problem is that the United States has failed to take full advantage of the regional institutions of which it is part – chiefly, the Organization of American States (OAS) and the Summit of the Americas – to advance a constructive hemispheric agenda. (An exception is the administration's commendable efforts to defend the inter-American human rights system.) True, in the new and changed context, working multilaterally is not easy. But doing so – in addition to forging stronger bilateral ties with key allies -- is essential to foster US interests and mobilize broader support. High-level consultations in pursuit of strategic goals in Latin America have been lacking. That is the best way to enhance US diplomatic clout and produce concrete results. It is hard to take frequent references to "partnership" seriously in the absence of such efforts.

---

[1] Inter-American Dialogue. "Remaking the Relationship,"
http://www.thedialogue.org/page.cfm?pageID=32&pubID=2925
[2] J. F. Hornbeck. "US-Latin America Trade and Investment in the 21st Century: What's Next for Deepening Integration?," http://thedialogue.org/page.cfm?pageID=32&pubID=3487

The costs of this deficiency, which has been building over several administrations, are manifest in the Venezuela crisis. Washington has limited leverage and options in responding to the troubling situation. To its credit, the Obama administration has expressed serious concern about the violence in Venezuela and has called on the government to respect human rights. The House of Representatives should also be applauded for its clear resolution in support of Venezuela's democracy.[3] But US effectiveness in dealing with the Venezuela crisis – along with other major policy challenges – is limited unless we are able to work in concert with our major hemispheric allies.

Unfortunately, so far most regional governments have been unwilling to take a forceful stand and apply pressure on the Venezuelan government. The problem is not a lack of instruments. On the contrary, OAS members have at their disposal among the most developed frameworks in the world to protect democracy. The Inter-American Democratic Charter and the OAS's original Charter are exemplary in this regard. The problem, rather, is the lack of political will to act in the current circumstances.

Venezuela, of course, is a special case. Since 1999, Hugo Chávez led a Bolivarian Revolution sustained by an oil bonanza that that spent lavishly throughout Latin America with the aim of curtailing US influence in the region. For both economic and political reasons, most Latin American governments are not prepared to criticize the government led by Chávez's successor, Nicolás Maduro. Member governments of ALBA, the political organization Chávez created in 2004, as well as Argentina, have expressed solidarity with the Venezuelan government.

It is worth emphasizing that, as an anti-US bloc, ALBA's strength has diminished in recent years. Even before Chávez's death in March 2013, ALBA had lost much of its political weight. That is chiefly because of the gravity of Venezuela's economic crisis, which has become more dire since Maduro took over. There is ample evidence that, out of sheer necessity, Venezuela is failing to meet a number of its commitments with ALBA members such as Ecuador.[4] And among many of the 18 members of Petrocaribe, Venezuela's development program that provides oil at discounted rates, there is disillusionment and even (in the case of Guatemala) withdrawal.

In recent years, in the second Bush administration and the first Obama administration, there were efforts to engage and ease tension with ALBA members like Venezuela, Ecuador and Bolivia. But such efforts bore scant fruit. They consumed limited diplomatic resources for Latin America and were thwarted. As a result, the Obama administration today is focused on deepening ties with more friendly governments in the region, such as Mexico, Colombia, Peru and Chile. Some progress has been made. But for different reasons, these governments, too, do not want to be out of step with their Latin American neighbors on the Venezuela crisis.

---

[3] Specifically, House Resolution 488

[4] Wall Street Journal, "Ecuador's Exports to Venezuela Plummet."
http://online.wsj.com/news/articles/SB10001424052702303563304579447382000518714?KEYWORDS=ecuador&mg=reno64-wsj

The Venezuelan case also exemplifies Latin America's growing ties with extra-hemispheric powers. China's economic role and presence in the region have been growing. China is the main trading partner with Brazil, Peru and Chile, and has expanding commercial relations with a number of other countries. Moreover, roughly half of China's $100 billion in loan financing to Latin America since 2005 has been directed to Venezuela. China's economic support for other ALBA members such as Ecuador is also significant.[5]

Of greater concern for US interests – and what bears close watching -- are the roles of Russia, and particularly Iran, in Latin America. Chávez was important in facilitating the entry of both countries in the region, especially given his personal and political affinity with Putin and Amadinejad. Russia's presence in the region to date has been modest, limited mainly to arms sales – over $14 billion over the past dozen years, about 75 percent of which was directed to Venezuela. The extent to which Russia is able to follow through on a recent statement by its defense minister about intentions to expand relationships with Cuba, Nicaragua, and Venezuela should be monitored carefully. Such a statement may, more than anything else, reflect posturing for domestic consumption. Given the state of its economy and other priorities, Russia's ability to become substantially more involved in Latin America is limited.

The United States also must continue to be vigilant regarding Iran's role in Latin America. In recent years, Iran has expanded its diplomatic presence in a number of countries. Its involvement in less benign activities should be followed carefully. In the early 1990s, there were two bombings against Jewish targets in Buenos Aires, Argentina, that have been attributed to the Islamic Shiite group Hezbollah. Although Hezbollah-related groups and Al Qaeda receive some financial support from sympathizers in Latin American countries (as they do in other countries), there is no evidence, as the State Department has reported, that these groups have operational cells in the region. There has been much speculation about more extensive involvement of Iran-related groups in Venezuela and elsewhere, though there has been no credible proof of threats.

Last November at the OAS, Secretary of State John Kerry was only recognizing reality when he declared the Monroe Doctrine formally dead. In fact, the Monroe Doctrine ended decades ago.[6] Extra-hemispheric actors have long been deeply involved in Latin America, and their involvement is bound to increase in coming years. There is little indication that such actors pose a serious danger or threat to US interests.

In addition, in the post-Chávez period, and in light of Venezuela's deepening economic crisis, the virulent strand of anti-American populism has lost some ground. This is not a moment for alarmism, but rather a realistic and sober appraisal of the challenges the US confronts in this hemisphere. US relations with most countries in the region, though disappointingly distant, are by and large cordial.

---

[5] Inter-American Dialogue, "China-Latin America Finance Database," http://thedialogue.org/map_list
[6] Michael Shifter, "Tras casi 200 años, era hora de enterrar la Doctrina Monroe,"
http://www.eltiempo.com/mundo/estados-unidos/ARTICULO-WEB-NEW_NOTA_INTERIOR-13220055.html

Still, the US needs to realize that there are serious risks of reduced engagement in Latin America:

First, the frustrating diplomacy surrounding the Venezuela crisis is illustrative of the new reality. The consequences of a possible implosion and spreading turmoil in Venezuela are serious and affect US interests.

Second, it is essential for the United States to pursue greater cooperation with Brazil, however difficult this might be in the short run. True, neither Brazil nor the United States is investing much in building confidence, especially in light of the Snowden affair, but this is critical for US relations with Latin America overall.

Third, the US needs to take better advantage of the propitious climate in Mexico for a reform agenda. The failure to deal effectively with the immigration question in the United States has serious costs for our relationship with Mexico (and other countries in the region as well) -- arguably our most important partner on a range of critical issues.

And finally, with security cooperation efforts yielding some benefits, US engagement should not be reduced in Latin America. Doing so would limit our ability to be helpful to our Central American and Caribbean friends in dealing with spreading criminality, which threats democratic governance and the rule of law.

Mr. SALMON. Thank you, Mr. Shifter.

I am going to yield myself 5 minutes to ask questions and then I will yield time to the ranking member.

Ambassador Reich, I would like to start with you. As Assistant Secretary for WHA in the early 2000s, what was your approach to developing strategy and policy to deal with countries in Latin America that were antagonistic to our interests and to democratic principles?

And if you were back in the chair today or at the NSC, what would be your top priorities in support of our interests in the region? And then finally, how would you instruct your diplomats on the ground to deal with the threats of expulsion we have seen in places like Ecuador and Bolivia?

Ambassador REICH. Yes, sir. I had a slightly different approach than the current administration. In fact, I had the advantage that I think the entire administration did. We did not preemptively give the other side anything they wanted.

In fact, quite the opposite. I will give you an example. The Cuban Government refused a visa for the person we had selected as the head of our interests section in Havana. They didn't give a reason. They just didn't like him and they weren't going to allow him in.

Instead of trying to reason with them, since I know, unfortunately, from personal experience a little bit about that government, I simply asked where the head of their interests section was. At the time, I was told that he was in Cuba on vacation and I said just simply tell them that he is not coming back. Forty-eight hours later we had the visa for our man in Havana.

Diplomacy is not just sitting down and talking to people. You can talk to your friends. We did talk to our friends. We had very good relations with our people.

Mr. Shifter correctly says—with our friends, I should say—that Colombia is an example of U.S. success, and it is bipartisan, by the way. I would like to say that it wasn't just the Republican administration behind Colombia that enabled Colombia to survive a Communist-supported, including Cuban-supported, insurgency over many years was made possible by both Democratic and the Republican administrations in the late '90s and in the 2000s.

We should deal with countries in the way that they deal with us. I mean, we have seen recently in Ukraine the error of trusting people who have other agendas than we think they have or even what they say.

The same thing applies in this hemisphere and there are many other examples that I can give you. What I would do today is I would support, for example, the resolutions in the House and Senate that would revoke the visas and freeze the accounts of those people responsible for the violence in Venezuela, and not only the government officials, but what the NSC spokesman said, the oligarchs in the case of Ukraine and Russia.

There are a lot of private-sector people in Venezuela and other countries in the region that have become billionaires, with a B, as a result of corruption from these left-wing anti-American populist governments that are in office.

They are investing their money in the United States. There are some of those people who have huge assets in the United States.

They come and they spend the weekends here. I don't understand why we allow that when their actions are undermining our national interests.

Mr. SALMON. One other question. I get really, really frustrated with the toothlessness of the OAS and I have heard testimony from the entire panel, and anybody that wants to address it, I would be interested in your thoughts as far as how do we motivate them to do the right thing.

I know we are paying about 40 percent of the funding for the OAS and we get little return, if any, and I don't know how we continue to justify this to the taxpayers. It looks just like we are throwing money down a rathole. They don't accomplish anything for us, and I would be interested in your thoughts.

Ambassador REICH. Again, my experience from having been in the U.S. Government for 15 years, including at international fora, although I prefer the bilateral rather than the multilateral relationship, is that we don't—we tend to treat governments who do things to us like we just had done—and I say we in this case, those governments that support democracy in the region—and I should say that in the case of not allowing María Corina Machado to speak at the OAS, if I am not mistaken—now, correct me if I am wrong—the United States, Canada and Chile and Panama—sorry, there were 11 countries—11 countries that supported Ms. Machado being able to speak, and there was precedent for this, I think we should support those countries.

The other 14, the countries of the English-speaking Caribbean with the exception of Barbados which abstained, which I personally don't think abstention is a very honorable course in this case but much more honorable than voting with the Government of Venezuela to shut up an elected representative of the people of Venezuela who represented the peaceful dissident movement, and the other countries—Brazil, Argentina and the others that sided with Venezuela—I think that we should not just deal with them on the multilateral forum.

Our Ambassador to the OAS should not be the only one that would express discontent with what they did. I think that there should be a cost to relations with the United States overall—economic relations. We are the most powerful economic nation in the world. There is a reason for that.

Our economy is based on freedom—individual freedom, free markets, individual initiative. That freedom is being destroyed by Venezuela, has been destroyed by Cuba, is being destroyed in other countries in the region—Nicaragua, Bolivia, Ecuador, et cetera.

I think we need to side with the countries that support freedom. We need to actively oppose the countries that destroy freedom, and whether they vote one way or another in a forum we should pay attention to that.

Mr. SALMON. Our fault. Mr. Duncan.

Mr. DUNCAN. Mr. Chairman, is an amen out of order there?

Mr. SALMON. I recognize Mr. Sires.

Mr. SIRES. Thank you, Mr. Chairman.

You know, the State Department's budget was cut. Now, in turn, we have a cut in the Western Hemisphere about 21 percent. How detrimental is that in dealing with the Western Hemisphere as we reduce money to be able to work with some of these countries? Anybody? Mr. Shifter.

Mr. SHIFTER. Thank you. I think it is, clearly, not helpful and it does undermine our ability and our capacity to act effectively.

There is no—and it is hard to put a number on it exactly to—but, certainly, and of course more than anything I think the amount of money it sends a message. Latin Americans see this.

They see that we are cutting, we are trimming, we are pulling back and I think that is not a reassuring message for our friends who want to see—who think that there is a lot at stake for the United States, the relationship deepen.

So I think it is a negative message and signal that is being sent. I understand why we need to cut budgets up here but that, I think, is a consequence and a reality that we need to deal with.

Mr. SIRES. Mr. Berman, what do you think some of the consequences will be?

Mr. BERMAN. It is a good question, sir, and I would like to, if I may, broaden the question beyond simply the State Department because I would note, and I noted in my written statement, that there has been what amounts to a substantial budgetary draw down on, for example, the operating budget and, as a result, the horizons of combatant commands like Southern Command.

Southern Command, the posture statements over the last several years, reflect a clear trend in which the acting commander at the time has said we are no longer in the business—and, obviously, I am paraphrasing—we are no longer in the business of competing and contesting the activities of actors such as Iran, for example, and South America.

We have essentially retracted northward and now sit in Central America and our concerns are mostly with arms trade and with narcotics trafficking. This is a preemptive, I may say, ceding of the battlefield if the understanding is that what Iran is doing, what Russia is doing—these are countries of particular concern, certainly, to this hearing—what they are doing in the region can be contested, can be diluted in its effectiveness if the United States is down there both in an economic sense but also in a military sense—in a concrete military sense.

And I think it is worth pointing out that this is a trend line that consumes not only the State Department but it is also one that is affecting the Defense Department as well with long-term effects for both our ability to see what is happening in the region but also to counteract it if we choose to do so.

Ambassador REICH. Mr. Sires, it is an important question. I hate to keep going back to my experience but I will take the opportunity since the question was asked by the chairman about what did I do. I happened to be the first Assistant Secretary for the Western Hemisphere after 9/11 and we had a serious reduction in our resources as a result of the fact that we had to move a lot of—we, the United States Government, moved people and money to where there was a war, logically, and I defended that publicly.

Resources are extremely important to the State Department, to our foreign policy establishment, but they are not everything. What I think is very important is to have the support of other parts of the government, to have the support of the President, the National

Security Council and again, understand the fact that we represent in those positions not just a department of the United States Government but we represent the entire United States and we should think of our resources in a more comprehensive way than just the limited budget that we have.

Mr. SIRES. Can somebody talk a little bit about what is the major obstacle preventing the OAS from being an effective organization?

Mr. SHIFTER. I will try. First of all, it is important to have some perspective. I think the OAS has always had more than its share of problems.

Mr. SIRES. They don't do anything.

Mr. SHIFTER. What?

Mr. SIRES. They don't seem to——

Mr. SHIFTER. But if you go back those are the criticisms, you know, 15 or 20 years ago about being irrelevant, not credible, marginal. Some of those same terms were used a long time ago.

I think the main obstacle, to answer your question directly, is that politically the hemisphere has changed a lot in the last 10 years. It is much more fragmented. It is much more polarized.

The OAS operates by consensus and it is very hard, and there was a consensus in the early 1990s at the end of the Cold War. The governments went from military governments to civilian governments. There was a move there when people came together supporting democracy and markets, and then things started to unravel. Chávez came in 1998.

He was a polarizing figure, and it is very hard for an organization that deals with that kind of politics unless you really get in there and fight and make deals, and I think the United States hasn't done as good a job as it should.

So, now, you could try to say the Secretary General could do a better job and you could point to other factors, and I am not denying that. But I think the main obstacle is just a very complicated landscape.

Just to finish, I spoke to the previous Secretary General in Colombia who was the President of Colombia, Cesar Gaviria, and asked him what he thought about the OAS. He said, you know, I was glad that I was in the OAS in the 1990s and not now because I think I would have a much harder time. He realizes the politics are much, much more difficult.

Mr. SIRES. So is it obsolete?

Mr. SHIFTER. I don't think it is obsolete. I think the United States has a role to play and I think the other countries have to step up.

But I think there has been a lack of political commitment and political engagement in doing the hard work of really making an effective organization. We have to understand we went through a big period with the Chávez thing.

Now I think we are entering a somewhat, even though we have this crisis in Venezuela we are entering, a different period. There aren't going to be these sort of super populist leaders. Maduro doesn't have the money that Chávez had. He can't do what Chávez did during that period.

Things have become more complicated. I think there's another opportunity. I think it is a mistake to give up on it. The United

States is not involved in any other multilateral organization in this hemisphere except the Summit of the Americas. As it has been mentioned, the United States is not a member of CELAC and MERCOSUR. I think we need to be part of these organizations and do the hard work to make them more effective.

Mr. SIRES. Can somebody talk to me a little bit about why it seems that Cuba has its tentacles everywhere and yet people are sceptical of the meaning behind these efforts that Cuba is making in all these countries? Can somebody talk a little bit about that?

Mr. CLAVER-CARONE. I can take that. In particular, because I think we have an opportunity right now and we are concerned about thinking forward. We are concerned about Russia.

We are concerned about Iran and we talk about all these things but there are current events and I think we can't underestimate enough what we are currently seeing in regards to, because I think it is a perfect example, the concern of inaction breeding impunity, and it is the shipment of weapons to North Korea.

This isn't just a small shipment of weapons to North Korea. As I mentioned, it is the largest amount of arms that has ever been interdicted to North Korea since the Security Council's resolution, the first time a nation in the Western Hemisphere has violated international norms.

This would have been the biggest shipment of MiGs to North Korea since 1999, a sale that Kazakhstan did, and it would have— these were mint condition RPGs that would have affected our forces, U.S. forces in Korea—put our guys in danger in Korea. This was the shipment that got caught, but even the U.N. panel of experts shows that things have gotten away.

If we, the United States, let this pass and essentially not do anything, and I understand that the current rationale of the State Department is that this is a multilateral issue since these are international sanctions, but if we are going to allow essentially the Security Council to have Russia decide what we are going to do in this regards. Obviously, China protects North Korea in that regards, nothing is going to happen.

And therefore, all of our concerns that we think about and anticipate in regards to Venezuela and Ecuador with Iran and with Syria, et cetera, Russia, et cetera, then the message right there that is sent, if United States doesn't say that this is unacceptable, something so egregious, the message that is going to be sent is at the end of the day we are always going to be protected from doing so and we are going to green light those activities in regards to our future concerns.

Mr. SIRES. Thank you, Mr. Chairman.

Mr. SALMON. Thank you. The Chair recognizes Mr. Duncan.

Mr. DUNCAN. Thank you, Mr. Chairman. Thanks for holding this hearing.

Ambassador Reich, your comments were spot on and I appreciated the last exchange. But how do we export freedom? And that is rhetorical, I know, but I think about Colombia, and when the gentleman from New Jersey and I were there back in the spring of 2012 at the Summit of the Americas we met with some members of the Colombian congress and I remember them saying, and I can't remember verbatim, but we talked about the economic prosperity that Colombia was experiencing.

And one thing they said were low taxes, limited government, free markets. And I said, wait a minute, that is the foundation of what this country was founded on, and they were getting it. They were actually saying just enough government to support the free market.

I thought that was amazing to hear that from a leader in another country telling me the principles that actually made America great. And so I would ask just take a minute. What should we or could we do to export the things you talked about earlier? What can we do?

Ambassador REICH. Well, for example, I would say, first of all. But even that is not enough. Going back a few years I think we made a mistake, I am going to make a personal judgment call, on doing away with the U.S. Information Agency.

There was a separate U.S. Information Agency. Yes, it probably wasn't as effective as it could have been. But rather than making it more effective, what was done was it was incorporated into the State Department with positions called public diplomacy positions.

As a result we don't have an open and overt information agency in the U.S. Government that talks about all the things that the United States does for the rest of the world.

One of the things that I think we should do besides setting an example for the fact that this economy works and free economies work and unfree economies do not work is we need to repeat that. It becomes very obvious.

People should know. They should look at Cuba. They should look at Venezuela. Venezuela has the largest oil reserves in the world. Venezuela should be one of the most prosperous countries in the world.

Today, the Venezuelan people are standing in line and housewives are literally fighting, fighting in supermarkets over a loaf of bread. Why? Because they are run by people who still believe in Marxism. After nearly 100 years of failures of systems based on Marxism you still have these people in Cuba, Venezuela, Ecuador, Bolivia, Nicaragua and other places trying to make it work.

It is not going to work. But we need to reinforce that. I think we have a responsibility as the leader of the free world to promote freedom much more actively.

Mr. DUNCAN. Well, it works for those that are in power and——

Ambassador REICH. Oh, absolutely.

Mr. DUNCAN [continuing]. They just continue pushing those policies because it supports their positions and their economic benefit.

Mr. Berman, last summer the State Department delivered a report to the U.S. Congress that essentially said that Iran's influence in Latin America is waning and it was a result of a piece of legislation that I passed.

However, in your testimony you suggest that in fact that is not the case, citing the warm and personal relationship that was formed between former President Chávez and Ahmadinejad.

Now that they are both exited from the stage, do you expect this close relationship to continue under Maduro and Rohani and if not what do you expect will be the net effect on Iran's long-term plans in Latin America?

I would just love to kind of start a dialogue about Iran. Is it still a threat here and can you speak of that?

Mr. BERMAN. I can, sir, and I would say speaking for myself I think it is absolutely still a threat and the dialogue over Iran with regard to its presence in the Americas is quite misleading because people tend to look at Iran's deliverables with regard to the region rather than Iranian intentions, and Iran has signed over 500 trade and cooperation pacts with the various countries of the region since it entrenched itself back in 2005 or began to entrench itself in 2005.

Most of those trade agreements and cooperation agreements save for the ones that it signed with Venezuela have been undelivered and they really remain unrealized, and as a result, people have taken to thinking that what Iran is doing is essentially simply a dalliance in the Americas.

And I would make the point that if you look at long-term Iranian strategy to use various regions including Latin America as a way to circumvent sanctions, which was very important to them up until last fall when they started the Geneva process, but I would argue it is still important to them now.

And looking at Latin America as an area where they can marshal support for a revisionist radical world view and garner the support of regional regimes and lessen their isolation that way, I think what you are seeing is an Iranian presence that is qualitatively and quantitatively far more significant than it was a decade ago and it is one that will continue as you look forward into the future because there are a number of strategic opportunities that Iran is likely to seize upon in coming years.

Mr. DUNCAN. I would say two decades ago, if you go back to the AMIA bombings in Buenos Aires. And so we have established the fact that you and I agree that Iran is a threat in this hemisphere so let me ask you this. What should the U.S. strategy be?

Mr. BERMAN. Well, sir, I think a good start would be to actually implement legislation that was passed and in this particular case I refer to the act that you sponsored, with regard to recognizing that there is a problem.

And as you know, where the U.S. discourse is with regard to Iran and Latin America is essentially frozen as of last summer. Last summer, I had the privilege of testifying before the House Homeland Security Committee on this precise issue, on where Iran's footprint in the region is, and I am sorry to say that we had just come off of a disclosure by the State Department of what was objectively, I think, a very feeble assessment of the intelligence surrounding what Iran has been doing in the region, and nothing has been done since because there was the August recess and then there was sequester and what have you.

And the aggregate result is that U.S. policy toward Latin America, with regard to Iran, is precisely where it was last summer. There isn't a strategy to go down there, to compete and contest and dilute in economic terms, in political terms, to rally sympathetic regional governments in sort of constellations like, for example, the Pacific Alliance that have the ability to dilute Iranian influence.

Latin America is still an open playing field for Iran and I think you are going to see in coming years that Iran is going to take full advantage of that playing field.

Mr. DUNCAN. All right. Well, my time is up. I appreciate that. I would love to delve into at future hearings or just in conversations, Mr. Chairman, about whether we need to mimic that piece of legislation now with regard to Russia and their involvement in this hemisphere. And with that, I will yield back.

Mr. SALMON. Thank you.

Mr. Meeks.

Mr. MEEKS. Thank you, Mr. Chairman, I don't know if I have any questions but maybe I will get through my statement because I want to make sure the record is clear where I stand.

Number one, I think the OAS is a very important organization. I think that we need to engage with the OAS now more than ever. Who is the OAS? It is one of our allies. Everyone is sitting there.

So if somebody dares say something that we don't like we are going to disassociate ourself with them and say that they don't need to exist anymore? That is part of the problem. Some of us would like to, Ambassador Reich, the same policy that we had 30 years ago and utilized them in South America you want to still use the same thing.

One man said if you believe the same way you believed 30 years ago today you have wasted 30 years. Things have changed. This world is a much smaller place today than it was 30 years ago.

There is more democracy—you want to talk about democracy? There is more democracy in South America today than there was 30 years ago. There are more countries that are electing Presidents and governments through a democratized process today than there were 30 and 40 years ago.

When we would prop up dictators, we propped them up for the benefit of our country, not thinking about others. We forget that history. Yes, I have got problems when people are not able to come up and stand and protest, as I said, at a recent hearing that took place on Venezuela.

I got problems because I know the history of me and my country. Just as I had problems when our Government struck down and beat individuals like my colleague, John Lewis, who sits in this Congress.

But if I thought the same way I thought back then 40 and 50 years ago I would have a big problem sitting here as a Member of Congress today. I had to recognize the changes and the differences, and so we need to do that also with Latin America. I was there.

I saw it earlier in 1998 when I got elected. I recognized what I saw when Hugo Chávez got elected. There was a bipartisan delegation of individuals who were down there talking, trying to work it out with policies, Ambassador Reich, that you could have said we don't like them.

And there was a coup d'etat clear and simple in Venezuela, and half an hour after it we recognized the coup government, not the government that was elected democratically.

Yet we say we love democracy. We have got to understand from which we come in this and try to figure out how we can work together to make a difference—this administration and the State Department.

I have yet to hear people talking about what are we doing and how we can make a difference. I heard Mr. Shifter say something that I thought was significant, that we are now living in a global economy and that our economies are connected.

No one talked about how we got Chile and Mexico and Peru all partnered with us in TPP. Nobody talks about how the fact or whether or not some of our allies—I heard someone shout down Brazil. Well, Brazil is a country that is developing and is great, has its own population, have a lot to give with reference to energy.

We have got to recognize that and not just say we got to—because they don't agree with us 100 percent we are going to put them away. We condemned, and I have problems with some of the decisions that President Morales of Bolivia has and the position that he has taken there.

But we never recognized that for the first time the people of Bolivia decided they would elect someone who is indigenous. And the people that he represents, the people of Bolivia and what their thought pattern was and is and to at least give them some semblance of respect that they democratically elected a President who looked like many people who had historically before that never been able to get involved and have a voice in their government. Those things have to be recognized.

We have to deal with those realities if in fact we are going to have a harmonious relationship here on this hemisphere. To listen to what I have been listening to thus far, we blame everything, the whole world and everything that is all wrong because of the influence that Cuba has on everything.

Yet we don't change anything. Nothing has changed, so that can't mean that it is a success. So we do the same thing over and over and over and over again and then complain and complain and complain. We should learn something so that we can get a different result instead of having it going over and over again.

No one talks about what we have had—well, somebody mentioned our good relationship with Colombia. Go talk to the President of Colombia and ask him what he thinks, since he is our good ally.

Ask him what he thinks we should do and how we should move. We can't do things bilaterally or unilaterally, rather. If we are going to resolve certain things we got to do things multilateral and that is why the OAS is tremendously important.

I know I am out of time and I wish I had a question. I had some but I want to make sure that I am clear on the record, and I will end as I began.

If we want to be serious about working with our neighbors to the south, we have got to do so in a different way, not as my way or the highway, not that I don't consider what you do or anything of that nature.

We have got to do it in a multilateral way in a way that is respectful. I end it with this. I remember President Clinton. He was leaving the presidency. I asked him what is the difference between what he thought was important when he got elected President and

when he left, and he said that, I don't care how small the country—
we could use our military might but that won't change them.

It is giving some respect and working together. Yes, we have got
the biggest military in the world and we know how to use it when
we need to.

But we have got to talk to folks and we got to figure out how
we do things in a multilateral way and not just do it unilaterally.

I yield back.

Mr. SALMON. I thank the gentleman.

I recognize the gentlewoman from Florida.

Ms. ROS-LEHTINEN. Thank you so much, Mr. Chairman, and I
apologize for my back and forth. We are doing some hallway ap-
pointments—democracy in action.

And coming from an enslaved Communist regime where my family had to flee, and 50 some years later we still don't have democracy, and the OAS remains as silent as it always has when it
comes to supporting democracy. I love getting interrupted by our
democratic process so I never mind scooting in and out of committee rooms.

Now, some would like to defend the OAS. I see it as a failed institution and I hurt that our money is going to this institution—
40 percent of its budget—and what did the OAS do just on Friday?

María Corina Machado, who has now been stripped of her legislative immunity, is a legislator in the National Congress. She was
invited by Panama to speak in favor of human rights and democracy. Can you imagine?

What nerve to speak in favor of democratic principles in the
OAS, and there is the Secretary General, a buffoon who just continues to silence the opposition, refuses to hear that there are any
problems—see no evil, hear no evil—and so they do nothing, and
this wasteful institution is gobbling up our money.

What an insult. The Obama administration would like us to believe that our region is stable and prosperous but it fails to acknowledge the ongoing threats to our national security, our stability and the challenges that we face in promoting democracy,
freedom, and the rule of law.

And, you know, a democracy is more than holding an election,
even a fraudulent election at that, because we had an election, free
and fair. Can you say that about the other countries that have had
elections? Really, Maduro?

I presented to Secretary Kerry evidence of the electoral fraud in
Maduro's case. Nothing has been done, and Ortega, he changes the
constitution so that he can get reelected. There is no separation of
powers. But a democracy is more than an election.

A democracy is ruling in a democratic way. It is making sure
that the opposition, the minority, has a voice. Maduro's acts are
those of a coward and a bully, and if the administration continues
to allow his actions to go not even talked about then it is only
going to embolden him.

Throughout the past 6 weeks we have witnessed this ongoing
democratic crisis in Venezuela go further and further and all we
hear from the Obama administration is words and hardly even
words, hardly even that.

Why? I thank the members of our committee who have co-sponsored a bill that would sanction those individuals who are committing human rights abuses in Venezuela. I am disappointed in the action of the OAS on Friday.

To see democracies like the Dominican Republic, Colombia, other democratic nations that are democracies because they govern in a democratic way making the mistake of siding with the repressive regime in Caracas, not in solidarity with the people who are yearning for democratic change, that hurts me extensively.

And we know about the ties between the Castro brothers and the Maduro regime. We have seen the Cuban troops who are there. More Cuban troops are coming every day. Military advisors are sent to Caracas to help Maduro oppress his own people.

I cited how many deaths have occurred. Who has got the arms in Venezuela? Is it the students or is it the national guard and all of the thugs of Maduro? If these violent acts were occurring in other regions, Mr. Chairman, I think that we would act. But we choose to do nothing in Latin America. I think these countries are hurt by their proximity to the United States.

Now, the President has correctly issued an executive order to sanction those in Russia who have undermined the democratic process and threatened the security of Ukraine. I applaud him for that.

But no similar order has been signed for Venezuela. Those officials in Venezuela are killing young people on the streets. There have been tortures happening in the prisons. Young people have disappeared, and at the beginning of the Ukraine crisis many observers might have missed this interesting footnote, Mr. Chairman—that the Russian defense minister stated that Russia was in discussion with eight foreign countries, seeking overseas military facilities including three in our own hemisphere—Cuba, Venezuela and Nicaragua.

And Russia continues to bolster its military in front of our faces. Last month the Russian spy ship—as we know, it was in the press—it was spotted allegedly in the Port of Havana. Just 2 years ago, a Russian submarine was spotted off Florida waters.

Russia had sent three navy ships to our region that were docked in Venezuela and Nicaragua in 2008, and in the earlier part of this decade the Russians withdrew from the Lourdes intelligence facility in Cuba, in my native homeland, but they can always come back.

And what about China? Not only is Russia there, not only is Cuba there but China is in Latin America as well. Chinese investors are looking to build a canal in Nicaragua where opponents believe that this tactic is just a way to funnel money to Daniel Ortega and his cronies.

And we see, as Mr. Berman had pointed out, Iran, Hezbollah, other foreign terrorist organizations that are using narco trafficking to fundraise with their illicit activities abroad.

So we can't properly address these issues if this administration does not put more resources and more attention to Latin America. We must not turn our back on the people of the Americas because this will allow rogue regimes to fill the void that American leadership has left behind.

So I wanted to ask the panelists, if I might, Mr. Chairman, about two issues—the North Korean ship from Cuba carrying illicit military equipment that was stopped by the Panamanians in the canal and the Colombian peace talks with the FARC that is taking place, in a bitter irony, in a state sponsor of terrorism country, Cuba.

And I am sorry if you had discussed those before while I was in and out.

Mr. CLAVER-CARONE. We did.

Ms. ROS-LEHTINEN. What was the conclusion?

Mr. CLAVER-CARONE. Very briefly, we keep speculating about all these issues that are upcoming whether it is Iran, whether it is Russia, et cetera, and we have an opportunity to draw a line, and the line that we are going to draw right now in regards to North Korea.

These shipments weren't, as I said, just a few arms that were being sent. It was the largest violation—I am sorry to be repetitive—the largest violation of U.N. sanctions to North Korea ever since it was——

Ms. ROS-LEHTINEN. What do you think is going to happen now that we know that and they have issued their interim report?

Mr. CLAVER-CARONE. The U.N. panel of experts took it to, obviously, now to the Security Council. They said that there was obviously a conscious violation of international sanctions and now the Security Council there is going to decide and they are going to see there are individual entities that should be sanctioned, et cetera.

Obviously, we know for a fact that the Cuban military's conglomerate, GAESA, had something to do with it because every single transaction that had to do with the shipment involved GAESA which, by the way, is headed by General Luis Alberto Rodriguez Lopez-Callejas, which is Raul Castro's son-in-law and runs the entire tourism industry in Cuba as well, which we are also continuing to feed into.

That being said, whether the U.N. Security Council is going to in any way sanction GAESA or any of these individuals, I wouldn't hold my breath. At the end of the day, as I mentioned, obviously, Russia plays a part in this.

China, which protects North Korea, plays a part in this. Thus, if the United States does not draw a line in the sand in regards to these weapons sales, which is extraordinarily egregious with the facts that I mentioned in my testimony, we are welcoming the speculation in regards to Russia, I should say.

Ms. ROS-LEHTINEN. Yes. And would you say that now I think the biggest problem that we might face is a move by some folks to take Cuba off the state sponsor of terrorism list?

They have sort of decided they don't have the votes because of a lot of the hard work that we have done in Congress and so now, lamentably, we didn't put that in Helms-Burton so that is a decision that is made by the executive branch.

That is why I worry about these Colombia peace talks with the FARC taking place in Cuba. If an agreement is reached it would be used by saying hey, Cuba is no longer a terrorist country because it was the site of this honeymoon even though they just broke international sanctions with North Korea with this illegal shipment of arms. Do you see the move now to take Cuba off the state sponsor of terrorism?

Mr. CLAVER-CARONE. Obviously, the biggest effort that is being made by folks that advocate normalized relations with Cuba is to take them off the state sponsor of terrorism list.

This is what is being pressed mostly because it is a unilateral decision of the President. But there is legislative guidance to it, and in the legislative guidance to it essentially what they would need to qualify is that there needs to be a commitment from the Cuban Government that the United States accepted that they would not be involved in any of these acts in the future.

Now, the fact that they have been caught red-handed and the fact that the U.N. panel of experts has shown that they have been involved in some of these shipments in the past and there is a lot of speculation into because there was a lot of these patterns, well, pretty much clearly shows that they cannot be trusted in that regards.

And in regards to the FARC, I would note that there was just recently indictments in Federal court in Virginia against other low-level FARC individuals who are now in Cuba as part of this extraordinarily large delegation.

Now, this delegation keeps getting larger and larger and larger with lower and lower-level officials because, you know, guess what, they are being indicted here in the United States for terrorism and for some egregious acts and now they are going to be in Cuba.

Are they going to ever come and face justice here? Probably unlikely. The fact as well that Joanne Chesimard was named to the top 10 most wanted terrorist list is what also makes it very difficult to justify their removal from that list. A recent BBC documentary on Gaddafi brought about—they refound, rekindled Frank Terpil. Who is Frank Terpil, many of you recall, was the rogue CIA agent who sold nuclear material, who led Gaddafi's hit squads and they interviewed him once again guess where? In Cuba.

Frank Terpil is still around and, obviously, we know what he did. So all these things adding up makes it, I think, would make it very difficult to justify the removal of Cuba from the state sponsor list.

Ms. ROS-LEHTINEN. Ambassador Reich.

Ambassador REICH. You are the chairman of the Western Hemisphere—I mean, sorry, the Middle East Subcommittee so—sorry about that, madam.

I think that, to make a comparison, to have the talks between the FARC and the Government of Colombia in Havana would be the media equivalent of having talks between Hamas and Israel in Tehran. That is about how much sense it makes.

Let me give you also an anecdote about Colombia that goes to a lot of the statements that have been made here, and I am very sorry that Mr. Meeks left because I really wanted to engage him in a little dialogue about some of the facts that he apparently has gotten wrong about what happened in Venezuela because I was Assistant Secretary when some of those things that he claims happened did not happen.

But on Colombia, in 1991 then President Bush 41 pulled me out of retirement, one of my many retirements, and asked me to go to the U.N. Human Rights Commission in Geneva. That was the year that the first Gulf War started.

In fact, it was the day that the first Gulf War started. We were trying to get the Latin American Governments, among other things—that was my job, several continents including Latin America—to support several human rights declarations. One of them was on Cuba.

The Colombian Ambassador to the Human Rights Commission and I became friends. Over a period of weeks I tried to lobby him to support a very simple resolution asking for a special rapporteur from the U.N. Human Rights Commission to examine the conditions of Cuban jails, which Castro has never allowed examination by international bodies.

And finally, after 4 weeks of lobbying him, he admitted—he lost his patience with me and in a very friendly manner said, you know, collega—he said, my colleague, he says, you know that Colombia could never accompany the United States in this project, as he called it, this resolution, he said, because you know what Fidel Castro is able to do and has done in my country. And I said what is that.

I knew, but I wanted to hear him say it. He says, he has killed, he has kidnapped, he has supported the terrorists. He says, we cannot vote against Cuba at the United Nations.

Now, I reported that. That is in the annals of the State Department somewhere in that huge warehouse where the Raiders of the Lost Ark is stored—or the Ark itself, I should say.

And in the files of the State Department there is that conversation and it is an incredible admission by a strong democratic government that they could not vote against Cuba, as he put it, even on a human rights resolution at a multilateral forum, and this is why, to go back to Mr. Sires' question why does the OAS not work?

Not because it is the OAS but because it is a multilateral forum and the countries' personalities change when they are surrounded by other diplomats who get together every afternoon and talk to each other day after day and have drinks and reinforce each other's prejudices, one of which is that they don't like the United States.

I, frankly, have to say that I am so happy I was never asked, except for that—twice the President asked me to go to Geneva for the Human Rights Commission.

I think multilateral fora are inherently corrupt, intellectually corrupt, and so that is why we need to do our effective diplomacy at the bilateral level.

Ms. ROS-LEHTINEN. They are afraid of Castro for that reason and Maduro they don't want to vote against him because they like the cheap or free gas.

Ambassador REICH. Again, Madam Chairman, I said in my remarks that Cuba is an organized crime state. It is run like the Mafia is run. When Castro doesn't like somebody, what they're doing to them—like for example, Pinera in Chile.

Pinera's problems with the student movement in Chile was not coincidental. It was aided and abetted by Castro as a way to keep Pinera from moving Chile too far to the center. After 20 years under the coalition of the socialists and the Christian Democrats, finally Sebastian Piñera, a conservative, was elected, and guess what?

All of a sudden there is all of these problems with the students that completely divert President Piñera's agenda from doing what he wanted to do. If you were to ask the CIA to give you information about Cuban involvement in the student movement rebellion, if you want to call it that, against Piñera, unfortunately, I am now out of the government so you can't share it with me but I would urge you to do that——

Ms. ROS-LEHTINEN. Thank you.

Ambassador REICH [continuing]. As well as other examples that I would be happy to tell you about.

Ms. ROS-LEHTINEN. And thank you, Mr. Ambassador. So sorry I ran over time. Thank you, Mr. Chairman. Thank you very much.

Mr. SALMON. You know what? This has been so important and so intriguing and we have got such a wonderful panel. I have not used the gavel at all today. I have let everybody go over.

It was an incredibly important issue that we talked about today. I continue to believe that we have woefully neglected this hemisphere and I share with the gentlewoman frustration with some of these multilateral organizations and I think, Ambassador Reich, you have summed up a lot of my feelings.

I think that a lot of these multilateral organizations are inherently corrupt in fact, not only do we not get value, it is actually counterproductive and it is very, very frustrating to me.

There is an old axiom that you either act or you are acted upon, and I think that right now, and you said it, Mr. Berman, that nature fills a vacuum. Nature abhors that vacuum and fills that vacuum. We have neglected the hemisphere.

I think foreign policy in general in the entire world has been neglected but here it is in our own neighborhood and it has been woefully neglected and someday we are going to pay the price.

I don't think anybody expected a few months ago that Russia would do what it did with Ukraine. We didn't expect that they would do what they did with Georgia.

But it has happened and it is happening, and if we keep falling asleep at the switch as we have been for the last several years, not just the United States but the world is going to pay a hell of a price, and that is why I have let everybody say what they said today and thank you and thank the panel.

And without any other business, this subcommittee is adjourned.

[Whereupon, at 4:49 p.m., the subcommittee was adjourned.]

APPENDIX

MATERIAL SUBMITTED FOR THE RECORD

SUBCOMMITTEE HEARING NOTICE
COMMITTEE ON FOREIGN AFFAIRS
U.S. HOUSE OF REPRESENTATIVES
WASHINGTON, DC 20515-6128

Subcommittee on the Western Hemisphere
Matt Salmon (R-AZ), Chairman

March 18, 2014

TO: **MEMBERS OF THE COMMITTEE ON FOREIGN AFFAIRS**

You are respectfully requested to attend an OPEN hearing of the Subcommittee on the Western Hemisphere, to be held in Room 2255 of the Rayburn House Office Building (and available live on the Committee website at http://www.ForeignAffairs.house.gov):

DATE: Tuesday, March 25, 2014

TIME: 2:00 p.m.

SUBJECT: U.S. Disengagement from Latin America: Compromised Security and Economic Interests

WITNESSES: The Honorable Otto J. Reich
President
Otto Reich Associates, LLC

Mr. Ilan I. Berman
Vice President
American Foreign Policy Council

Mr. Mauricio Claver-Carone
Executive Director
Cuba Democracy Advocates

Mr. Michael Shifter
President
Inter-American Dialogue

By Direction of the Chairman

The Committee on Foreign Affairs seeks to make its facilities accessible to persons with disabilities. If you are in need of special accommodations, please call 202/225-5021 at least four business days in advance of the event, whenever practicable. Questions with regard to special accommodations in general (including availability of Committee materials in alternative formats and assistive listening devices) may be directed to the Committee.

COMMITTEE ON FOREIGN AFFAIRS

MINUTES OF SUBCOMMITTEE ON _____ *the Western Hemisphere* _____ HEARING

Day___ *Tuesday*___ Date_____ *03/25/3014*_____ Room____ *2255 RHOB*____

Starting Time ___ *3:10 p.m.*___ Ending Time ___ *4:49 p.m.*___

Recesses _____ (_____ to _____) (_____ to _____) (_____ to _____) (_____ to _____) (_____ to _____) (_____ to _____)

Presiding Member(s)

Chairman Matt Salmon

Check all of the following that apply:

Open Session ☑ Electronically Recorded (taped) ☐
Executive (closed) Session ☐ Stenographic Record ☑
Televised ☐

TITLE OF HEARING:

"U.S. Disengagement from Latin America: Compromised Security and Economic Interests"

SUBCOMMITTEE MEMBERS PRESENT:

Chairman Matt Salmon, Ranking Member Albio Sires, Rep. Ileana Ros-Lehtinen, Rep. Gregory Meeks, Rep. Jeff Duncan

---

NON-SUBCOMMITTEE MEMBERS PRESENT: *(Mark with an * if they are not members of full committee.)*

N/A

HEARING WITNESSES: Same as meeting notice attached? Yes ☑ No ☐
(If "no", please list below and include title, agency, department, or organization.)

STATEMENTS FOR THE RECORD: *(List any statements submitted for the record.)*

N/A

TIME SCHEDULED TO RECONVENE _____
or
TIME ADJOURNED ___ *4:49 p.m.*___

Subcommittee Staff Director

www.ingramcontent.com/pod-product-compliance
Lightning Source LLC
Chambersburg PA
CBHW080527290526
45790CB00006B/2325